NIC

LONDON PUB GUIDE

Nicholson
An Imprint of HarperCollins*Publishers*

A Nicholson Guide

© Nicholson 1994

First published 1981
5th edition 1994

Illustrations by Claire Littlejohn
Design by Bob Vickers

London street maps
© Nicholson, generated from the
Bartholomew London Digital Database

London Underground Map by
permission of London Regional Transport
LRT Registered User No 94/1496

All other maps
© Nicholson

Nicholson
HarperCollins*Publishers*
77-85 Fulham Palace Road
Hammersmith
London W6 8JB

Great care has been taken throughout this book to be accurate,
but the publishers cannot accept responsibility for any errors or
their consequences.

Produced by HarperCollins, Hong Kong

ISBN 0 7028 2515 8

81/5/68

CONTENTS

The George, Strand

INTRODUCTION

The British pub is an institution which has evolved from the Saxon alehouse, the medieval tavern and inn, to the Victorian 'public house'. For centuries London was one of the great brewing capitals; in the 11thC the Domesday Book recorded that the monks of St Paul's Cathedral brewed 67,000 gallons of ale annually. In the 12thC children drank beer as a preventative to typhoid. In 1437 a Brewers' Company was set up and many breweries were established alongside the Thames. In the 16thC workmen's wives blended malt, yeast, water and sugar at home. By the end of the 17thC there was a switch from unhopped, heavy and sweet ale to lighter and more bitter hopped beer. By 1733 there were almost 100 gin shops (drinking houses) in St Giles next to tuppenny brothels. A publican's placard in Southwark promised: 'Drunk for 1d. Dead drunk for 2d. Clean straw for nothing'. The rise of gin palaces resulted from the Beerhouse Act of 1830 which permitted the unlicensed sale of beer. Throngs of gin palace patrons spurred the brewers into improving their premises and it was out of these gin mills, taverns and inns that London's 7000 pubs evolved.

The British pub has always been a great meeting place and a venue for games (such as darts and dominoes) and entertainment (Shakespeare presented his plays in taverns, and Music Hall was born in Victorian pubs). Today, London's thriving fringe theatre, alternative comedy and live music scene is largely based in pubs.

The variety of London's pubs is enormous; historic pubs in the City, modern pubs of unusual design and decor, riverside pubs, theatre pubs.

All pubs serve beer, spirits and wines. Real ale, brewed in the traditional manner, is served in numerous London pubs, thanks largely to the endeavours of the Campaign for Real Ale (CAMRA) whose annual *Good Beer Guide* should be consulted for a full list.

Pub food offers excellent value for money. Many pubs serve snacks and hot food at lunchtime and in the evening, and a few have restaurants.

This guide has been divided into two main sections; pubs by area and pubs with special features. Each entry has information on the pub's history, character, the brewer to which it is allied, and availability of food and entertainment. There are also sections on bars, wine bars, brasseries and cafés.

SYMBOLS & ABBREVIATIONS

B – bar food (from a snack to a full meal)
L – restaurant lunch
D – restaurant dinner

(Reserve) – advisable to reserve a table in the restaurant

● – *open all day 11.00-23.00 Mon-Sat, 12.00-14.00 & 19.00-22.30 Sun.*

Where there is no ● symbol the pub is *open traditional pub hours: 11.00-15.00 & 17.30-23.00 Mon-Sat, 12.00-14.00 & 19.00-22.30 Sun.*

Any other variations to the above hours are stated at the end of each entry.

Opening and closing times refer to the pub.

THE BREWERIES

In the first edition of the *London Pub Guide,* we attempted to credit each pub with the brewery it was tied to. However, this proved confusing in the case of some of the big national combines whose pubs are grouped under trading names unfamiliar to most readers – whose only concern, we believe, is 'what beer does it serve?' So, with apologies to those combines who really prefer their full and proper names to be used, we have simply answered that obvious question. For example, if a pub is tied to *Watney Combe Reid Truman* and is designated a 'London Host Group' pub, we have simply put *Watneys* since that's whose beer you will be drinking. *Semi-Free Houses* are also tied to a particular brewer but serve other beers as well.

PUBS BY AREA

CENTRAL LONDON
BLOOMSBURY & HOLBORN

W1, NW1, WC1, WC2. Bordered by Tottenham Court Road, New Oxford Street, High Holborn, Gray's Inn Road and Euston Road.

Bloomsbury has always been a favourite area for writers, artists and musicians. Its two great focal points are the University of London and the huge columned edifice of the British Museum which houses countless treasured antiquities.

Holborn, too, has connections with learning; the area has always been popular with lawyers who found it convenient for the Inns of Court. Gray's Inn, one of the four great Inns of Court, is within its boundaries, and another, Lincoln's Inn, lies just south of High Holborn.

Original London Walks run *A Literary London Pub Walk* which takes you on a literary trail through the handsome Georgian squares of Bloomsbury, visiting historic old pubs which were once frequented by Dickens, Thackeray, Wilde and Shaw. *Phone 071-624 3978 for details.*

Tubes: Tottenham Court Road, Holborn, Chancery Lane, Russell Square, King's Cross, Euston, Warren Street, Goodge Street.

🍺 Bricklayer's Arms   6 G5
31 Gresse St W1. 071-636 5593. *Samuel Smith.* Pleasing design; the craftsman-made joinery and brick bars won this pub a CAMRA award for the best pub refurbishment in the country. Two tap rooms below, elegant lounge above, real ales and good bar lunches. **B**

Calthorpe Arms   7 C3
252 Gray's Inn Rd WC1. 071-278 4732. *Youngs.* Friendly small bar popular with businessmen at lunchtime and with locals in the evening and at weekends. Has rather a grim history; the Brinks-Mat robbery of 1984 was allegedly planned in the bar, and it was here that the first policeman in London was killed. **B L**

🍺 Cittie of Yorke   7 C4
22-23 High Holborn WC1. 071-242 7670. *Samuel Smith.* On the site of what was once a medieval pub then a 17th-century coffee house. Under the vaulted ceiling is one of the longest bars in London and cosy cubicles where lawyers used to have confidential chats with their clients. The triangular coal-burning stove is still in use but appears to have no chimney (the answer

to the mystery is that the flue runs under the floor). Main hall and downstairs cellar bar both serve excellent bar food. Old Brewery Bitter and Museum Ale. *Closed Sun.* **B**

Hercules Pillars
7 B5

18 Great Queen St WC2. 071-242 2218. *Watneys.* Civilised modern pub rebuilt in the '70s. Elegant surroundings – lots of mirrors and brocade. Interesting buffet bar and real ales. Popular with businessmen. *Closed Sun eve.* **B**

The Lamb
7 C3

94 Lamb's Conduit St WC1. 071-405 0713. *Youngs.* A sumptuous Victorian local pub in the heart of Bloomsbury. Photographs of music hall stars and prints of old London decorate the wood-panelled walls. Still has the original cut-glass swivelling snob screens once used to separate the gentry from the servants. Now has a pleasing mix of customers, good home-cooked food from the corner servery and a small rear patio. Roast lunches on *Sun.* **B L**

The Lamb

Museum Tavern
7 B4

49 Great Russell St WC1. 071-242 8987. *Free House.* Located opposite the British Museum, this traditional tavern attracts a mixture of research students and sightseers. Karl Marx drank here while he was working on *Das Kapital* in the reading room

of the British Library. Victorian interior, with traditional cast-iron tables, engraved glass windows and ornate carvings behind the bar. Very crowded at lunchtime. Afternoon cream teas served. *Open all day Sun.* **B**

🍺 Old Red Lion   7 B5
72 High Holborn WC1. 071-405 1748. *Charrington.* Rather proud of the fact that Oliver Cromwell's headless body spent a short time within its walls after he was beheaded. Despite this gruesome note, it's a nice old bar with lots of woodwork, engraved glass and windows. Upstairs is the pleasant Cromwell Bar. *Closed Sat & Sun.* **B**

🍺 Peter's Bar   7 B4
Bloomsbury Park Hotel, 126 Southampton Row WC1. 071-405 2006. *Free House.* Although part of a hotel, Peter's Bar has the feel of a real pub. The cellar bar has open fires and lots of mahogany, oak and blackened beams. Virginia Woolf was a former patron. Good selection of bottled lager. Basket meals and bar snacks. *Open all day Mon-Fri. Closed Sat lunchtime & all day Sun.*

🍺 The Plough   7 B4
27 Museum St WC1. 071-636 7964. *Taylor Walker.* Edwardian literary pub, popular with publishers and writers, as befits its Bloomsbury location. Long bar with wood panelling, dim lighting and Tiffany shades. Lounge and family room. Outdoor tables. **B**

🍺 Princess Louise   7 B5
208 High Holborn WC1. 071-405 8816. *Free House.* A fine example of Victorian pub architecture decorated in heavy dark mahogany, with warm lighting, polished brass, glazed tiles and engraved glass. The gents toilet is even the subject of a separate architectural protection order! A good range of ales. Excellent Thai food in the upstairs bar. *Open traditional hours Sat & all day Sun.* **B**

🍺 Ship Tavern   7 C5
12 Gate St, off Lincoln's Inn Fields WC2. 071-405 1992. *Youngers.* In an alley leading from High Holborn to Lincoln's Inn Fields. The oldest parts, including the cellar with its blocked-off priest's hole, are 16th century. Catholic priests used to come here to say the then forbidden Mass and could escape the forces of the law by hiding in the cellar. Full of legal types from nearby Lincoln's Inn Fields. Separate restaurant does grills and steaks. *Closed Sat & Sun.* **B L** *(Reserve)*

● **Sun Inn**   **7 C3**
63 Lamb's Conduit St WC1. 071-405 8278. *Clifton Inns*. Small, bustling and rumbustious with an exceptional choice of real ales. Vaulted cellars under the streets store up to 70 real ales; 20 are available at any one time. **B**

The Thunderer   **7 D3**
59 Mount Pleasant WC1. 071-837 6114. *Free House*. Just on the other side of Gray's Inn Road, and virtually next door to the Post Office Headquarters. The theme is *The Times* newspaper, known as *The Thunderer* in days of past glory; photographs and old editions cover the walls. Flicks Wine Bar upstairs. **B L D**

● **White Horse**   **7 C5**
St Clement's Lane, off Portugal St WC2. 071-242 5518. *Whitbread*. Decorated in old-world style, this is a darts and real ale pub. Serves Boddingtons, Greene King Abbot Ale and Wethereds Bitter. *Closed Sat eve & all day Sun.* **B**

STRAND & FLEET STREET

WC2, EC4. From Charing Cross Station to Ludgate Circus.

Originally a bridle path running alongside the Thames, the Strand is now home to pubs, restaurants, hotels, theatres, shops and offices. It extends from Charing Cross to the Law Courts (Royal Courts of Justice) which front onto the Strand itself and unite all four Inns of Court – Middle and Inner Temple, Lincoln's Inn and Gray's Inn. From here you enter the City of London through the two dragon guardians at the western end of Fleet Street.

Fleet Street extends eastwards from Temple Bar to Ludgate Circus, and has always been associated with printing and publishing. The character of Fleet Street has changed as the office and printing works of the national newspapers have almost all moved out, yet the name will probably remain synonymous with 'the press' for a long time to come. This is an intriguing area of concealed alleys and courts with the River Fleet flowing through a conduit beneath.

Traditionally, barristers and journalists have frequented the pubs in this area at *lunchtime* and in the *early evening*. By about *21.00,* the 'wigs and pens' and numerous local office workers have departed and some of the pubs close early. *Note that several are closed for all or part of the weekend.*

Tubes: Charing Cross, Aldwych, Chancery Lane, Blackfriars.

The Cartoonist   7 D5
76 Shoe Lane EC4. 071-353 2828. *Courage*. In the old heart of
the newspaper world, this Victorian pub is the headquarters of
the International Cartoonist Club. The sign outside is changed
every year, the design being chosen from those submitted by
cartoonists. Inside is lavishly wallpapered with original cartoons.
Home-cooked food. Barbecues in *summer*. *Closed Sat & Sun*. **B**

Cheshire Cheese   7 D6
5 Little Essex St, off Milford Lane WC2. 071-836 2347.
Courage. Not to be confused with its Fleet Street neighbour, Ye
Olde Cheshire Cheese (see below). This is an intimate Jacobean
pub with original oak beams and three bars; the Millers Bar for
wine, snacks, and coffee and biscuits in the morning, the
saloon bar for real ale and down to the Dive Bar for bottled
beers, spirits and hot lunches. Popular with the legal profession
from the nearby Law Courts. Reputedly haunted by an
inhospitable ghost which spends its nights moving an
enormously heavy fruit machine across the saloon bar door.
Closed Sat & Sun. **B**

Cheshire Cheese, Ye Olde   7 D5
Wine Office Court, 145 Fleet St EC4. 071-353 6170. *Samuel
Smith*. Rebuilt after the Great Fire of London in 1666, this

Ye Olde Cheshire Cheese

somewhat rambling building has a low-ceilinged interior, six bars and three small restaurants, all with oak tables and sawdust floors. Past regulars include Dr Samuel Johnson, Pope, Voltaire and Charles Dickens, who mentioned it in *A Tale of Two Cities*. The 14th-century crypt of Whitefriars Monastery is still intact beneath the cellar bar. Old Brewery Bitter and Museum Ale. Famous for good, rich game puddings. **B L D** *(Reserve)*

Coal Hole 7 B6

91 Strand WC2. 071-836 7503. *Nicholson's.* Right next to the Savoy, this pub has a ground floor bar and a basement wine bar. In the 19th century it was a meeting place for the coal-heavers who worked the Thames, and it was also the Wolf Club, founded by the actor Edmund Kean for repressed husbands who were not allowed to sing in the bath! Original features – etched glass, mirrors, bench seating and a long wooden bar. **B**

Cock Tavern, Ye Olde 7 D5

22 Fleet St EC4. 071-353 8570. *Courage.* This tavern originally stood across the road in Apollo Court, but was transferred to

Ye Olde Cock Tavern

its present site in the mid 1880s. All that is left of the original pub is its sign, which is said to have been carved by Grinling Gibbons. Literary associations; Thackeray, Dickens, Tennyson and Pepys all drank here. Nowadays, lawyers and nearby office workers frequent the place. Pictures of 18th-century London adorn the walls. Large dining room specialises in roasts, puddings and pies. *Closed Sat & Sun.* **B L** *(Reserve)*

Devereux   7 D6
20 Devereux Court, off Essex St, off Strand WC2. 071-583 4562. *Courage.* Tucked away off the Strand near the Law Courts and Middle Temple, this was first the town house of Robert Devereux, Earl of Essex, then a coffee house, now a pub. Busy with members of the legal profession, often in full regalia, in the brief lunchtime recess from Middle Temple. Restaurant serves English food. *Open to 21.30 Mon-Wed. Closed Sat & Sun.* **B L** *(Reserve)*

Edgar Wallace   7 D6
40 Essex St, off Strand WC2. 071-353 3120. *Whitbread.* Used to be called The Essex Head, which took its name from Robert Devereux, Earl of Essex. Dr Johnson founded the Essex Head Club here in 1783. Renamed in 1975, the year of the centenary of the birth of the crime writer Edgar Wallace. Copies of his books, relevant pictures, and framed personal letters, mostly donated by his daughter, decorate the walls. There is a good à la carte menu in the small restaurant upstairs. *Closed Sat & Sun.* **B L**

The George   7 D5
213 Strand WC2. 071-353 9238. *Charrington.* Tall and imposing timbered inn opposite the Royal Courts of Justice. Marks the point where Fleet Street ends and the Strand begins. Though the sign shows George III, it is actually named after the George who owned it when it was a coffee house in the 18th century. Bare boards, beamed ceiling and a long wooden bar. Carvery upstairs. Popular with members of the legal profession and tourists. *Closed Sat eve & all day Sun.* **B L** *(Reserve)*

Hogshead   11 C1
23 Wellington St WC2. 071-836 6930. *Whitbread.* Formerly the Gilbert & Sullivan. The original pub, in John Adam Street, was damaged by fire in 1979, so the photographs, playbills and musical scores of operas were moved here. The Gallery bar/restaurant serves full meals which are excellent value. 13 real ales. **B L D**

The George

🍺 **Lyceum**   **7 C6**
354 Strand WC2. 071-836 7155. *Samuel Smith*. There's a traditional tap room downstairs and an upstairs lounge with good
views over the Strand. A passage connects the pub to what
was the Lyceum Theatre, where Sir Henry Irving once declaimed
on stage. Real ale and good bar lunches. **B**

🍺 **Old Bell Tavern**   **7 D5**
95 Fleet St EC4. 071-583 0070. *Free House*. Built by Sir
Christopher Wren in 1670 to house and serve the workmen
rebuilding St Bride's Church, which had been badly damaged in
the Great Fire. Single U-shaped bar is made cosy with seating
nooks, old flagstones and beams. Small, friendly and unpreten-
tious. Five real ales on draught. *Closed Sat & Sun*. **B**

🍺 **Printer's Devil**   **7 D5**
98 Fetter Lane EC4. 071-242 2239. *Whitbread*. Takes its title
from the traditional nickname for a printer's apprentice (though
the sign shows a 'real' devil at a press). Notable collection of
early prints and etchings illustrate the history of printing. Pizza
restaurant upstairs. *Closed Sat & Sun*. **B**

Punch Tavern   7 D5

99 Fleet St EC4. 071-353 6658. *Nicholson's*. Named after the famous satirical *Punch* magazine which was conceived here by a group of radical journalists in 1841. The choice of title was inspired by the Punch & Judy shows which in those days used to enliven nearby Ludgate Circus. Original *Punch* drawings and cartoons adorn the walls. Vast etched mirrors. **B**

Seven Stars   7 C5

53 Carey St WC2. 071-242 8521. *Courage*. Between the Law Courts and Lincoln's Inn Fields stands this early 17th-century pub, one of the smallest in London. It is also one of the few pubs in the area which survived the Great Fire. One end of the bar is dedicated to a past customer – Charles Dickens – with caricatures of his characters. Full of barristers and other members of the legal profession. *Closed Sat & Sun*. **B**

Sherlock Holmes   11 B2

10 Northumberland St WC2. 071-930 2644. *Whitbread*. A good starting point for a pub crawl down the Strand. It used to be the Northumberland Arms where Sir Arthur Conan Doyle 'arranged' the first meeting between Sir Henry Baskerville and Sherlock Holmes in *The Hound of the Baskervilles*. In 1957 it changed its name and took the fictitious detective and his creator as its theme. The bar is full of relics from his famous cases. Upstairs is a perfect reconstruction of Holmes' study at 221b Baker Street, installed in 1953. Traditional afternoon teas served. **B L D** *(Reserve)*

White Swan   7 D6

28-30 Tudor St EC4. 071-353 5596. *Courage*. Very much a local pub, which used to be frequented by journalists and was affectionately known as the Mucky Duck. Gets busy at lunchtime with solicitors and barristers from the nearby Law Courts. *Closed Sat & Sun*. **B**

Witness Box   7 D6

36 Tudor St EC4. 071-353 6427. *Courage*. Built in 1974 in the cellar of a modern office block, though the bar is decorated in authentic Edwardian style. A show-piece for crime reporters, the walls are covered with cuttings on notable criminal events. The pub itself awards a plaque to the reporter whose crime story is voted best of the year. Excellent food – everything freshly cooked on the premises. Upstairs wine bar. *Closed Sat & Sun*. **B**

COVENT GARDEN

WC2. Bordered by Charing Cross Road, Strand, Kingsway and Long Acre.

When the famous fruit and vegetable market relocated to Nine Elms, the market building at Covent Garden was converted into small units, most of which are now specialist shops and eating places. The area is a flourishing centre for arts, crafts and designer knick-knacks, with market stalls, craft shops, boutiques and gift emporia all around the piazza and in the narrow streets and alleys nearby. The piazza itself is always lively with buskers putting on street performances of anything from South American music on native flutes to juggling and acrobatics. North of Long Acre, Neal's Yard and the Thomas Neal Centre offer a mixture of wholefood warehouses and art and fashion shops.

Covent Garden is also famous as a theatre district, and in fact it was the theatres which influenced the number of inns and coffee houses that sprang up in the 18th century. Today there are still many traditional pubs which are always lively with patrons from the nearby theatres and the Royal Opera House.

Tubes: Covent Garden, Leicester Square, Charing Cross.

🍺 Chandos   7 B6
29 St Martin's Lane WC2. 071-836 1401. *Samuel Smith.* Next to the English National Opera on St Martin's Lane, this huge Victorian pub has been restored to its former glory. The large ground floor bar has wooden floors and panelled alcoves, while upstairs is more comfortable with large leather sofas, deep cushioned window seats and an open fire. You can eat breakfast here from *09.00* and they also serve afternoon tea. *Open all day Sun.* **B**

🍺 Kemble's Head   7 B5
61 Long Acre WC2. 071-836 4845. *Courage.* A Victorian, gas-lit, ex-coffee house, named after John Philip Kemble, the actor-manager who once ran the Theatre Royal in Drury Lane. Decorated with prints and pictures of old theatres and of the man himself. Upstairs restaurant serves traditional English food. **B L D**

🍺 Lamb & Flag   7 B6
33 Rose St, off Garrick St WC2. 071-497 9504. *Courage.* A 300-year-old pub, frequented by Dickens, this is the only

Lamb & Flag

timber-framed Tudor building remaining in the West End. Originally known as The Bucket of Blood because of the bare fist fights that used to be staged in the upstairs room. Downstairs could be rough too – Dryden got the once-over in the alley outside for writing satirical verses about Louise, Charles II's mistress. Excellent range of cheeses and pâtés, all served with French bread. **B**

🍺 **Marquess of Anglesey**   **7 B5**
39 Bow St WC2. 071-240 3216. *Youngs.* A serious drinker's pub with a chequered history. It was changed from inn to coffee house in the 18th century, converted back to a pub in the 19th century, extended in 1858, demolished in the Blitz of 1941, and rebuilt in 1953 in traditional style. The home-cooked food served in the upstairs restaurant has become a feature of the place. **B L D**

🍺 **Marquis of Granby**   **7 B6**
51-52 Chandos Pl WC2. 071-836 7657. *Taylor Walker.* Pleasant pub round the back of Trafalgar Square. This is where the Bow Street Runners caught up with Claude Duval, the famous highwayman, who was eventually hanged at Tyburn. Very busy in the evenings. Hot food and two real ales. *Open all day Sun.* **B**

Nag's Head 7 B6

10 James St, off Long Acre WC2. 071-836 4678. *McMullens of Hertford*. This lively Edwardian pub is the London flagship of the above, old-established brewers. Strong theatrical flavour – old playbills adorn the walls. There are two real ales, two Hertford-brewed lagers, draught Guinness and home-made lunches. **B**

Nell of Old Drury 11 C1

29 Catherine St WC2. 071-836 5328. *Courage*. Opposite the Theatre Royal, Drury Lane, this charming pub with its bow-fronted windows and great atmosphere is one of the oldest in Covent Garden. Named after Nell Gwynne, an actress and mistress of Charles II. She was born in an alley off Drury Lane and sold oranges at the Theatre Royal before her talents were spotted by the king. There is even an intermission bell in the pub, and a tunnel once connected the pub to the theatre. **B**

Nell of Old Drury

Opera Tavern 11 C1

23 Catherine St WC2. 071-836 7321. *Taylor Walker*. Opposite the Theatre Royal, Drury Lane, this charming pub is popular with actors from the nearby theatres. Decorated with playbills

and photographs of stars past and present who have appeared at the Theatre Royal. When bottles rattle in the cellar some say it is caused by the vibration of passing traffic, others that it is the ghost of a man murdered and buried down there at the beginning of the century! Pre- and post-theatre suppers. *Closed Sun lunchtime.* **B**

Punch & Judy 7 B6

Covent Garden Market WC2. *Courage.* Opened towards the end of 1980 near the site of the first recorded Punch & Judy performance. Pub sign and pictures reflect the theme of the name. Watch street performers from the first floor balcony which overlooks the piazza. Flagstoned basement with wines, Directors and Best Bitter. **B**

Punch & Judy

☕ Sun Tavern 7 B5

66 Long Acre WC2. 071-836 4520. *Watneys.* Little Bacchus heads, draped in grapes, peer at you from the façade as you approach. Inside, the bar is furnished in comfortable pub Victoriana, with red plush and polished woodwork.

The Sun Tavern

Bacchus Wine Bar upstairs. Home-cooked meals. **B** *(not Sun eve)*

Two Brewers 7 B5
40 Monmouth St WC2. 071-836 7395. *Courage.* Small, friendly pub frequented by theatre-goers and tourists. The oak-panelled walls are lined with theatre programmes and playbills. Many years ago, when it was called The Sheep's Head, a freshly severed sheep's head was hung outside daily. *Closed Sun.* **B**

White Hart 7 B5
191 Drury Lane WC2. 071-242 3135. *Charrington.* Reputed to be the oldest pub in Covent Garden, it certainly holds the oldest licence in London (1201). Extensively restored but with its history kept intact. Cosy seating area at the back. **B** *(not Sat & Sun)*

White Swan 7 B6
14 New Row WC2. 071-836 3291. *Charrington.* Housed in an attractive Queen Anne building. The front bar is decorated with old mirrors and prints. The back bar is oak-panelled and hung with engravings. Pepys and Dickens reputedly drank here. *Closed Sun.* **B** *(not Sat)*

SOHO, PICCADILLY & LEICESTER SQUARE

W1, WC2. Soho is surrounded by Regent Street, Oxford Street and Charing Cross Road and is separated from Piccadilly Circus and Leicester Square by Shaftesbury Avenue.

Soho takes its name from the hunting cry of the 1600s, 'So ho', which the huntsmen would exclaim once they caught a glimpse of their quarry. It is now one of London's most cosmopolitan areas, an exciting square mile of pubs, bars, restaurants, nightclubs and specialist shops. This cosmopolitan identity has been cultivated by generations of immigrants who have left their mark by opening restaurants, delicatessens and pâtisseries. Chinatown, centred around Gerrard Street, is the centre of Britain's Chinese community. The area is also popular with the artistic community and the film and music industries. Attempts have been made to clean up the area and the gradual demise of pornography has helped, though some strip joints and 'hostess' bars still exist. Most people, though, come here for the colourful streetlife and varied nightlife.

Piccadilly Circus is the confluence of five major thoroughfares: Regent Street, Piccadilly, Shaftesbury Avenue, Lower Regent Street and Haymarket. It is most famous for its bright neon flashing signs depicting advertising slogans, and for the statue of Eros, dating from 1893.

Leicester Square's principal attractions are its cinemas, huge picture palaces which replaced the Victorian entertainment halls.

Shaftesbury Avenue is the heart of London's theatreland. Live theatre has flourished in the capital for more than four centuries since the first playhouse went up in 1576 and that great theatrical tradition is still much in evidence today along this bustling street which stretches from Piccadilly Circus to Bloomsbury.

Tubes: Oxford Circus, Tottenham Court Road, Leicester Square, Piccadilly Circus.

🍺 Argyll Arms   6 F5
18 Argyll St W1. 071-734 6117. *Free House.* Built in 1868, though there has been a tavern on this site for over three hundred years. Fine Victoriana; the four downstairs bars and one upstairs bar glitter with magnificent mirrors and decorated glass, set in genuine mahogany. The old manager's pulpit-like office still stands in the middle of the pub. Serves five real

The Argyll Arms

ales, and a good selection of wines in the Palladium Bar. *Closed Sun.* **B**

Blue Posts   **6 G6**
28 Rupert St W1. 071-437 1415. *Whitbread.* Named after the blue posts which stood outside taverns in the 18th century to advertise the local sedan chair service. A 1900 reconstruction with a mock Georgian façade. Inside is decorated with original oil paintings. Rupert Court, next to the pub, used to be a private passageway to stables belonging to the pub when it was an old coaching inn. Always crowded with tourists, office workers and pre-theatre drinkers. Excellent Irish coffee. Home-cooked food. **B**

The Clachan   **6 F6**
34 Kingly St W1. 071-734 2659. *Nicholson's.* Clachan is Gaelic for small village, but this is hardly a rural drinking spot, being only a few steps from the bustle of Regent and Carnaby Streets. It has been lavishly restored by the brewers. An unusual glass roof at the back has stained-glass images of Scottish soldiers in Highland dress. The vast circular bar serves both food and drink. **B** *(not Sun)*

Coach & Horses   **6 F5**
1 Great Marlborough St W1. 071-437 3282. *Whitbread.* Mid-

18th-century coaching inn on what was once the road to Bath. You can sit outside on pavement benches in summer. There are eight traditional ales including Flowers, Greene King Abbot Ale, Marston's Pedigree. Upstairs wine bar, The Horse Box. *Closed Sun.* **B**

🍺 Crown & Two Chairmen   6 G5
31 Dean St W1. 071-437 8192. *Nicholson's.* Earned its name nearly 200 years ago by playing host to royalty who arrived by sedan chair – a crown carried by two chairmen. Real ale, cocktails, hot and cold bar food. *Closed Sun.* **B**

🍺 De Hems   6 G6
11 Macclesfield St, off Shaftesbury Ave W1. 071-437 2494. *Taylor Walker.* During World War II this pub was a refuge for members of the Dutch Resistance. It's a big pub with a keen Dutch ambience. The name is Dutch for windmill and the wood-panelled walls are covered with Dutch Old Master prints. It's the only pub in London to serve Oranjeboom – Dutch lager – directly imported from Holland. They also specialise in Dutch snacks. The front of the pub opens out in summer to allow for outdoor drinking. Live comedy *Wed eve.* **B**

🍺 Devonshire Arms   6 G6
17 Denman St, off Shaftesbury Ave W1. 071-437 2445. *Courage.* Modernised old place with mock-Georgian dimpled windows. Main bar has dark oak furniture and sawdust on the floor. Lounge bar upstairs. Four real ales to choose from. **B**

🍺 Dog & Trumpet   6 F5
38 Great Marlborough St W1. 071-437 5559. *Taylor Walker.* A brash, lively place at the top of Carnaby Street. Used to be called the Marlborough Head but changed its name to the Dog & Trumpet (the world-famous logo of HMV records) in memory of the recording industry which flourished in the swinging '60s. Old wind-up gramophones decorate the back bar. **B**

🍺 French House   6 G5
49 Dean St W1. 071-437 2799. *Courage.* In 1914 this small pub was taken over by the first Frenchman to hold a publican's licence in England. It was the London centre for the Free French during the war. De Gaulle drank here and so, in their day, did Brendan Behan and Dylan Thomas. It has long been the favoured haunt of artists, actors and sporting stars, many of whose signed photographs adorn the walls. Champagne, pink or white, available in half bottles, is more popular than beer here, and there's an excellent selection of French aperitifs. There is even an antique dispenser for adding water to your Pernod. **B L D** *(not Sun)*

The Glassblower   6 F6
42 Glasshouse St W1. 071-734 8547. *Courage.* An old building with lots of untreated rough wooden beams, plain wooden settles and stools, and sawdust on smart wooden floorboards. Upstairs is a spacious, plush and comfortable lounge where food is served *at lunchtime.* **B L**

John Snow   6 F5
39 Broadwick St W1. 071-437 1344. *Watneys.* Took its name when the original John Snow pub, opposite, was demolished. The man himself was a surgeon whose research into water-borne disease helped rid Soho of an outbreak of cholera in the early 19th century. The image of the village water pump, source of all the trouble, is said to reappear outside the pub from time to time. Pool room and bar upstairs.

Old Coffee House   6 F6
49 Beak St W1. 071-437 2197. *Courage.* Quite a few London pubs began life as coffee houses in the 18th century – this is one that chose not to change its name when it ceased to serve the 'devil's brew', as coffee was once called. Long narrow panelled bar. Restaurant upstairs. **B L D** *(not Sat & Sun)*

The Salisbury

The Salisbury   7 B6
90 St Martin's Lane WC2. 071-836 5863. *Ind Coope.* Situated right in the heart of theatreland, a large Edwardian pub with beautiful etched windows. Inside, glittering cut-glass mirrors, gleaming polished brass and glowing red plush. Frequented by actors from the nearby theatres. Excellent and reasonably priced food. **B**

Tom Cribb   6 G6
36 Panton St, off Haymarket SW1. 071-839 6536. *Charrington.* Named after the 17th-century fist fighter, who ran it in the

days when it was the Union Tavern. Then it was a sporting pub, with cockfights in the cellar – now the haunt of businessmen and theatre-goers. Still remembers its past, with boxing prints around the walls. Made its film debut in *Fanny by Gaslight*. **B**

MAYFAIR

W1. Bounded by Piccadilly, Regent Street, Oxford Street and Park Lane.

The name comes from the Fair that was held here every May for many years in the 17th century. For a fortnight the streets would be alive with drunken revellers and prostitutes. Once the annual Fair was shut down, the village became respectable and since then Mayfair has been a classy, fashionable area of London.

Mayfair is where most of the smart hotels stand – the May Fair itself, Claridge's, the Dorchester, the Hilton and the Ritz just the other side of Piccadilly. Mayfair is also where you will find the Royal Academy, the Museum of Mankind, and Sotheby's, as well as shops selling expensive clothes and jewellery, Persian rugs and paintings.

Lending extra colour to the area is Shepherd Market, a little village with narrow streets and tiny houses from which the area developed with its annual May Fair!

Tubes: Hyde Park Corner, Green Park, Bond Street, Marble Arch.

🍺 **The Audley**   **10 D1**
41 Mount St W1. 071-499 1843. *Courage*. Pleasant Victorian pub, very popular with tourists. English restaurant upstairs; Oliver's Wine Bar downstairs. Three real ales and a buffet bar. **B L D**

🍺 **Burlington Bertie**   **10 F1**
21 Old Burlington St W1. 071-437 8355. *Charrington*. Traditional, smart pub with pictures on its walls of the famous music hall stars who sang about Burlington Bertie, famous for rising at 10.30. IPA and good food. *Closed Sat & Sun*. **B**

🍺 **Grapes, Ye**   **10 E2**
16 Shepherd Market, off White Horse St W1. 071-629 4989. *Free House*. Built in 1882, this traditional pub is situated right in the heart of Shepherd Market. Inside is traditional Victoriana and there is a genuine 19th-century open coal fire. Upstairs is a restaurant, The Vinery, which serves international food. **B D**

Guinea
10 E1

30 Bruton Pl W1. 071-409 1728. *Youngs.* Dating back to 1423, this pleasant old pub is hidden away in a narrow mews off Berkeley Square. Originally known as the One Pound One, a name probably suggested by a cattle pound which is thought to have stood nearby when this area was all farmland. Guinea was added in the reign of Charles II when the gold coin of the same name was first minted. Good but pricey restaurant. *Closed Sun.* **B L** *(not Sat)* **D** *(Reserve)*

King's Arms
10 E2

2 Shepherd Market, off White Horse St W1. 071-6290083. *Free House.* Lively pub with bare timbers and a dimly-lit gallery from where you can look down on the other customers. Charles Wells Bombardier, Everards Tiger, Wadworth's 6X and Webster's Yorkshire are the ales. *Open traditional hours Sat.* **B**

Red Lion
10 E2

Waverton St W1. 071-499 1307. *Courage.* Lovely 17th-century inn with a forecourt for summertime drinking. Subdued interior divided into small sections, with old paintings and prints of London, including a copy of a Canaletto. A copy of the day's *Financial Times* is always displayed at eye level in the gents' toilet! Restaurant is expensive and serves English food. *Open traditional hours Sat.* **B L D** *(Reserve)*

The Red Lion

● **Rose & Crown**   **10 E2**
2 Old Park Lane W1. 071-499 1980. *Courage*. 200-year-old country-style pub now surrounded by Park Lane residences. Said to be haunted by the ghosts of those hanged at Tyburn gallows (now Marble Arch) who were sometimes incarcerated overnight in the cellars here and apparently returned later in spirit. **B**

● **Running Footman**   **10 E2**
5 Charles St W1. 071-499 2988. *Courage*. Pub whose full name was once the longest in London – 'I am the only Running Footman'. A plaque on the wall explains the task of a footman – to run before his master's carriage clearing the way and paying the tolls. Victorian decor – mahogany panelling and engraved mirrors. Popular with hotel staff and croupiers from the nearby clubs. Four real ales. A la carte restaurant upstairs serves traditional English food. *Open all day in summer*. **B L** *(not Sat)* **D**

● **Shepherd's Tavern**   **10 E2**
50 Hertford St W1. 071-499 3017. *Courage*. An elegant, 18th-century pub in Shepherd Market. Georgian bow windows, panelled in Canadian pine. Much favoured by the RAF and Allied Forces during World War II. Amongst the old relics you'll find the Duke of Cumberland's sedan chair which has been converted into a telephone box. Downstairs there are real ales and bar snacks. Upstairs restaurant serves English food. **B L D**

KNIGHTSBRIDGE & BELGRAVIA

SW1, SW3, SW7. A two-part area, bordered by Kensington Road and Knightsbridge to the north, Grosvenor Place and Buckingham Palace Road to the east, and to the south by a crooked line formed by Sloane Street, Pont Street, Beauchamp Place and the Cromwell Road.

Knightsbridge was, like so many other built-up parts of London, originally a tiny village, famous for its taverns, duels and highwaymen. Through it flowed the River Westbourne (now underground) and it was on a bridge at this stretch of the river where knights would duel or fight, hence the area's name. The Great Exhibition of 1851 transformed Knightsbridge, bringing wealth to the area, which has remained ever since and can be seen in the high-fashion and luxury shops.

In the days of the knights, Belgravia was rather different too – a fog-bound swamp patrolled by brigands. Today it is a stately residential area of squares and terraces, Regency mansions and foreign embassies.

Original London Walks run *An Aristocratic London Pub Walk* which explores the squares and cobbled backstreets of Belgravia, stopping at historic inns and pubs along the way. *Phone 071-624 3978 for details.*

Tubes: Hyde Park Corner, Knightsbridge, Sloane Square, Victoria.

The Antelope
10 D5
22 Eaton Ter SW1. 071-730 7781. *Taylor Walker.* Old-fashioned pub, established in 1780 when the area was rural. Popular with locals and tourists alike; always crowded in the evening. Upstairs restaurant. **B L**

Duke of Wellington
63 Eaton Ter SW1. 071-730 3103. *Whitbread.* Traditional English pub on the borders of Chelsea and Belgravia. There has been a pub on this site for more than 250 years. The interior is warm and welcoming. Red lamps, military prints and a copper bar top. Pictures of the Iron Duke abound. Tables outside. Reputation for excellent Guinness. **B** *(not Sun)*

Ennismore Arms
10 B4
2 Ennismore Mews SW7. 071-584 0440. *Courage.* Homely, relaxing pub in a cobbled mews. Period Georgian decor, an open fire, comfortable seating and good home-cooked meals. **B**

The Grenadier

Grenadier
10 D3
18 Wilton Row SW1. 071-235 3074. *Watneys.* Tucked away in a mews behind Hyde Park Corner, this pub is steeped in military tradition. It was once an Officers' Mess for the Duke of Wellington's soldiers, and it was from here that the Grenadiers

marched off to Waterloo in 1815. Full of military bric-à-brac; there is a sentry box outside and the Duke's own mounting block in the passageway at the side. Reputed to be haunted by an officer caught cheating at cards and accidentally flogged to death. Famous for its Bloody Marys, shaken to order to a secret recipe. English restaurant. **B L D** (Reserve)

Nag's Head   10 D3
53 Kinnerton St SW1. 071-235 1135. Youngs. Looks like a tiny corner shop from outside; it is small, cosy and cottagey inside. Took its name from the stables surrounding it which are now mews properties. Attractive 19th-century handpumps. Gets very crowded in the evening. Open all day Wed-Fri. **B L D**

☛ Paxton's Head   10 C3
153 Knightsbridge SW1. 071-589 6627. Taylor Walker. Opposite the Knightsbridge entrance to Hyde Park, this restored Victorian pub is named after Sir Joseph Paxton, designer of the original Crystal Palace which stood nearby. Two bars in the Victorian-style interior, one a large island bar and the other a simpler brick construction. Closed Sun. **B**

Star Tavern   10 D4
6 Belgrave Mews West SW1. 071-235 3019. Fuller's. Small and friendly traditional pub in a delightful cobbled mews.

The Star Tavern

Comfortable surroundings; mahogany tables, upholstered settles and ceiling fans. Open fires in both bars. Decorated with artefacts of the imperial tea and coffee trade with the Orient. Always busy at lunchtimes and in the early evening, but has a local feel outside of these times. *Open all day Fri.* **B** *(not Sat & Sun)*

● **Tattersall's Tavern** 10 C3
2 Knightsbridge Green SW1. 071-584 7122. *Scottish & Newcastle.* Built on the former site of Tattersall's auction rooms, this pub preserves the memory of their long association with racing. The bar has sporting prints of famous horses and race meetings, and there is a replica of the Tattersall yard pump – the original of which is in the paddock at Newmarket. *Closed Sun.* **B**

● **Wilton Arms** 10 D3
71 Kinnerton St SW1. 071-235 4854. *Whitbread.* A charming little mews pub in Edwardian style with delightful little alcoves in which to enjoy a quiet drink. The spirits are kept in timber bars. Brasswork and old ornaments everywhere. There's a conservatory at the back with a colourful painted wall and hanging plants. **B**

WESTMINSTER, WHITEHALL & ST JAMES'S

SW1. Bordered by Piccadilly, Haymarket, Whitehall, Millbank, Vauxhall Bridge Road and Grosvenor Place.

Westminster begins at Whitehall, a wide, elegant thoroughfare which stretches from Trafalgar Square in the north, past Downing Street towards Parliament Square, Westminster Abbey and the Houses of Parliament, seat of British Government. The area is rich in tradition, pageantry and history and has played an integral part in the development of parliamentary democracy.

St James's is an area famous for its park and its gentlemen's clubs. St James's Park and Green Park, divided by the Mall, were acquired by Henry VIII in 1532. St James's Palace is still the official court to which foreign ambassadors are accredited.

Tubes: Green Park, Piccadilly Circus, Charing Cross, Embankment, Westminster, St James's Park, Victoria.

● **Blue Posts** 10 F2
6 Bennet St, off Arlington St SW1. 071-493 3350. *Courage.* Lord Byron used to live next door to this charming traditional pub. There would have been blue posts in the old courtyard here to advertise the local sedan chair service. Inside is an original sedan chair. Restaurant upstairs. *Closed Sat & Sun.* **L D** *(Reserve)*

● Buckingham Arms   **10 F4**
62 Petty France SW1. 071-222 3386. *Youngs.* Busy mid-Victorian pub. The walls are hung with prints associated with the Duke of Buckingham. Popular with businessmen. Excellent home-cooked food. *Closed Sat eve.* **B**

Chequers   **10 F2**
16 Duke St SW1. 071-930 4007. *Courage.* Small, friendly pub based on the idea of past and present Prime Ministers, whose country retreat is Chequers in Buckinghamshire. It was the first pub to be built after the Great Fire of London. *Closed Sun.* **B**

● Clarence   **11 B2**
53 Whitehall SW1. 071-930 4808. *Courage.* There's a preservation order on this 18th-century house with its gaslights inside and out, sawdust floors, wooden pews and tables. Popular with Civil Servants from the nearby Ministries. There are six real ales, and regular 'guest' beers. An entertainer performs *four nights a week.* **B L**

● Golden Lion   **10 F2**
25 King St SW1. 071-930 7227. *Nicholson's.* Built next to the old St James's Theatre in 1832, this pub has many theatrical associations. Lillie Langtry used to drink here. Ornate exterior with large rounded windows and lamps. Tetley, Marston's Pedigree and Best Bitter from handpumps. Excellent food in the restaurant. *Open traditional hours Sat. Closed Sun.* **B L**

● Old Star & Crown   **10 G4**
66 Broadway SW1. 071-222 8755. *Whitbread.* Used to be nicknamed The Cab House when it was a regular stopping-off point for drivers of horse-drawn hansoms – and some present-day cabbies still call it that. Popular with employees from the Houses of Parliament, the Home Office and New Scotland Yard. Downstairs is the Crown Vaults wine bar. *Closed Sat & Sun.* **B**

● Red Lion   **10 F2**
23 Crown Passage, off King St SW1. 071-930 4141. *Courage.* A charming pub in an 18th-century backstreet. The site once supported a hospital for 'leprous maidens', and it is also said that there were secret passages linking the tavern with the nearby St James's Palace, down which Henry VIII could escape for an evening's revelry. This passage is also the site of the last duel fought on English soil. Home-cooked food in the restaurant upstairs. *Open traditional hours Sat. Closed Sun eve.* **B L**

● Red Lion   **10 F2**
2 Duke of York St SW1. 071-930 2030. *Nicholson's.* A little

gem of a Victorian gin palace with rich mahogany panelling and beautifully preserved mirrors, each engraved with a different British flower. Always packed; the pavement outside becomes an extension of the bar. Four traditional ales and home-cooked food. **B**

Silver Cross 11 B2

33 Whitehall SW1. 071-930 8350. *Courage.* 13th-century building with a preservation order on its fine Tudor waggon-vaulted ceiling. It was licensed as a brothel by Charles I and has been a tavern since 1674 – but no one has got around to revoking (or making use of) the brothel licence. A Tudor maiden, whose portrait is on the wall, haunts the upper floor. Home-cooked food in a pleasant and friendly atmosphere. **B**

Two Chairmen 11 A2

Warwick House St, off Cockspur St SW1. 071-930 1166. *Courage.* This charming pub was built in 1683 and was reconstructed during Queen Victoria's era. The Two Chairmen are sedan chair carriers of the 17th and 18th centuries, not senior executives. Very friendly atmosphere. *Closed Sun.* **B**

Two Chairmen 10 G3

39 Dartmouth St SW1. 071-222 8694. *Courage.* A small, cosy pub with low ceilings and dark oak panelling. Originally built as

The Two Chairmen, Dartmouth Street

a coffee house, it was named after the sedan chair carriers who plied their trade during the 17th and 18th centuries. *Closed Sat & Sun.* **B L**

🍺 **Westminster Arms**   **10 G3**
9 Storey's Gate SW1. 071-222 8520. *Free House.* An imposing pub on three floors displaying the coat of arms of the family of the Dukes of Westminster. Big Ben bar downstairs aims to be a typical English inn and serves several real ales. So popular with MPs that it has a division bell to summon them back to vote. Queen Anne restaurant upstairs, Storey's Wine Bar in the basement. **B L**

VICTORIA & PIMLICO

SW1. Bounded by Buckingham Palace Road, Victoria Street, Horseferry Road and the Thames.

Victoria is dominated by Victoria rail, coach and underground stations, which accounts for the fact that many of the large old houses here have been turned into small hotels to accommodate the transient population. Victoria Street is clogged with office buildings and government departments, but is notable for Westminster Cathedral, built in 1903, which serves as the headquarters of the Roman Catholic church in the United Kingdom.

Pimlico was mostly built in the 1850s. It is now mainly a residential area with a plethora of restaurants, wine bars and antique shops, and two key attractions: down by the Thames, on Millbank, stands the Tate Gallery, the home of the principal collection of British art and modern painting; and in the top corner of the area stands Buckingham Palace.

Tubes: Victoria, Pimlico.

🍺 **The Albert**   **10 F4**
52 Victoria St SW1. 071-222 5577. *Scottish & Newcastle.* Grand, imposing Victorian pub positively gleaming with polished wood and fitted with original gas lamps and engraved glass windows. Upstairs, past portraits of Prime Ministers, is an excellent restaurant serving traditional English roasts and boasting an extensive wine list. Breakfast is also served between *08.00-10.30 Mon-Fri.* This handsome pub is popular with MPs (there's a divisional bell in the restaurant) and is close to New Scotland Yard. **B L D** *(Reserve)*

🍺 **Barley Mow**   **11 A5**
104 Horseferry Rd SW1. 071-222 2330. *Watneys.* Cosy pub with fine collection of Hogarth prints. An open fire in winter

The Barley Mow

and outside seating in summer in a very pretty area with red awnings, shrubs and garden furniture. This is the local pub for Westminster Hospital. Restaurant is open *weekday lunchtimes.* **B L** *(Reserve)*

📖 **Cask & Glass**   **10 F4**
39 Palace St SW1. 071-834 7630. *Shepherd Neame.* Intimate 19th-century pub – has the appearance of a dolls' house from outside, with its hanging baskets, window boxes full of flowers and white patio furniture. Very comfortable and pleasant inside. Renowned for its sandwiches. **B**

The Cask & Glass

Colonies   10 F4
25 Wilfred St SW1. 071-834 1407. *Courage*. Small pub converted in the '70s into a nostalgic corner for old colonials. Full of photographs of outposts of the lost Empire, the heads of stags and antelopes, and sundry spears and whips. *Closed Sat & Sun eve*. **B**

Fox & Hounds   10 D6
29 Passmore St SW1. 071-730 6367. *Charrington*. A truly old-fashioned one-bar beer house which was the last in London to get a spirit licence. Intimate interior; dark wood furniture and old prints. A very friendly local. **B**

🍺 Lord High Admiral   10 F5
43 Vauxhall Bridge Rd SW1. 071-828 3727. *Ind Coope*. Busy, modern, split-level pub which replaced an older one of the same name. Tables at the front and a large green at the back (which belongs to the nearby estate, but you can take your drinks there). Always full of young tourists. *Open traditional hours Sat*.

🍺 Morpeth Arms   11 B5
58 Millbank SW1. 071-834 6442. *Youngs*. Attractive riverside pub near the Tate Gallery. The cellars here are connected to an old tunnel which was used by prisoners to escape from the Millbank Penitentiary (now the entrance to the Tate) to avoid being shipped to Australia. *Open all day Sun in summer*. **B**

🍺 Rising Sun   14 D1
46 Ebury Bridge Rd SW1. 071-730 4088. *Youngs*. Handy for Victoria rail and coach stations and so attracting a cosmopolitan crowd, plus bandsmen from the Brigade of Guards. Nautical decor with model boats, prints and decorative plates. *Open traditional hours Sat*. **B**

WATERLOO & THE SOUTH BANK

SE1. Waterloo's main feature is the huge station, built in 1848, which serves the south-west London suburbs and south-west England. The huge entrance arch is a monument to the thousands of railway employees killed in action during World War I.

The South Bank Centre is a starkly modern cultural complex on the south bank of the Thames with a superb view of old London across the river. Started in 1951 with the Royal Festival Hall, the complex is now home to the Royal National Theatre, the National Film Theatre, the Queen Elizabeth Hall, the Purcell Room, the Hayward Gallery and the Museum of the Moving Image. There are restaurants, cafés and bars within the complex and also free events in the foyer which range from art exhibitions to modern jazz.

Also included in this section are some pubs in Southwark, an area further down the river, parts of which go back 2000 years. It was once the entrance to the City from the south and therefore several coaching inns were built in the area. Of these, the George Inn (see below) still stands. Southwark has always had a reputation for good, strong beer, made with Thames water. In fact Bankside was once described as a 'continued ale house'. Redevelopment of the riverside in this area has resulted in complexes such as Gabriel's Wharf, Hay's Galleria and Butler's Wharf, all of which house speciality shops and places to eat and drink.

Tubes: Waterloo, Borough, Elephant & Castle, London Bridge.

The Anchor   11 F2
34 Park St, Bankside SE1. 071-407 1577. *Courage*. An inn with a wealth of historical associations. The original pub on this site was frequented by a hideous mixture of smugglers, press gangs and warders from The Clink, a notorious prison nearby. Shakespeare's Globe Theatre and the bear pits and brothels of Bankside also attracted a lot of custom to the area. It was destroyed in the fire of 1666, and the present building was built in 1750. Dr Johnson lived here while he was compiling his dictionary and a first edition of the famous lexicon is on display. A maze of five small bars and two formal dining areas nestle at various levels with exposed beams, open fires, and nooks and crannies full of antique bric-à-brac. Excellent riverside views from the terrace and barbecue area. **B L D** *(Reserve)*

Founders Arms   11 E2
52 Hopton St, Bankside SE1. 071-928 1899. *Youngs*. A former pub of the same name was built on the site of the foundry where the bells of St Paul's were cast. This is a successful modern pub with fabulous views across the river to St Paul's itself from a glass wall at the back. Salad bar and à la carte restaurant. Traditional Sunday lunch. Beer from the famous brewery up the river. **B L D** *(not Sun)*

George Inn   11 G2
77 Borough High St SE1. 071-407 2056. *Whitbread*. London's only galleried coaching inn to remain intact. First mentioned in John Stow's *History of London* in 1590 and rebuilt after fire damage in 1676 to exactly the original plans. Patronised by Shakespeare and Dickens, who used the pub as the setting for many of his novels. There are two bars, a wine bar and an à la carte restaurant. The pub is set around a courtyard where there are occasional performances of Shakespeare. **B L D** *(not Sun) (Reserve)*

Goose & Firkin   11 E4
47 Borough Rd SE1. 071-403 3590. *Firkin Brewery*. The first of

the chain of Firkin real ale pubs, this is a friendly place with cockney sing-alongs around the piano at weekends. Goose, Borough Bitter, Dogbolter and sometimes the intensely powerful Gobstopper are on the pumps. *Open all day Sat.* **B**

🍺 Horniman   12 B2
Hay's Galleria, Battle Bridge Lane SE1. 071-407 3611. *Free House.* An ambitiously designed pub named in honour of the tea-trading family who traded here when this was the hub of London's dockside activity. Ornate woodwork and polished brasswork. Bar food, tea and coffee served all day. Patio for summer drinking. Great views of Tower Bridge and the river, with *HMS Belfast* directly alongside. **B L D** *(Reserve)*

🍺 Old Thameside Inn   11 G2
St Mary Overy Wharf, off Clink St SE1. 071-403 4253. *Nicholson's.* This inn has wonderful views over the Thames to the National Westminster Tower. The main bar has dark beams, pews and flagstones, and staff in black waistcoats. Waterside terrace. **B**

Old Thameside Inn

🍺 Wellington Tavern   11 D3
81-83 Waterloo Rd SE1. 071-928 6083. *Free House.* Not surprisingly, the Wellington Tavern is decorated with murals of the Battle of Waterloo.There are six real ales to choose from – Adnams, Toby, Yorkshire, Ruddles County, Youngs and Boddingtons. Handy for Waterloo, the Old Vic Theatre and the South Bank Centre. This is London's first-ever sign-language pub; deaf drinkers meet here *every alternate Fri eve. Open traditional hours Sat in winter.* **B**

NORTH & NORTH WEST LONDON
MARYLEBONE

W1, NW1. Bounded west and east by Edgware Road and Great Portland Street, to the south by Oxford Street and to the north by Regent's Park and St John's Wood Road.

That Marylebone was designed as a residential area is obvious from its attractive and imposing squares. Cutting north-south through the area is Baker Street where Sherlock Holmes was supposed to have roomed with the amiable Dr Watson. Further east in Harley Street the specialist doctors have their consulting rooms. Nearby is Wigmore Street with its concert hall where, by tradition, musicians make their London debut. Bustling Oxford Street is internationally known for its shops and department stores. Another important central artery of the area is Marylebone High Street with its designer clothes shops, classy food stores and continental-style cafés. Broadcasting House, the headquarters of the BBC, stands at the bottom of Portland Place.

Tubes: Marble Arch, Bond Street, Oxford Circus, Great Portland Street, Regent's Park, Baker Street, Marylebone, Edgware Road.

Allsop Arms   6 C3
137 Gloucester Pl NW1. 071-723 5864. *Courage*. The original house on this site was the entrance to the first cricket ground opened by Thomas Lord. Friendly pub with comfortable furnishings. Directors and Wadworth's 6X on tap. Benches and tables on the wide pavement outside. **B**

The Angel   6 D5
37 Thayer St W1. 071-486 7763. *Samuel Smith*. Timbered building on the corner of Marylebone High Street. Highly decorative Victorian interior with bars on two levels. Bench tables outside. *Open traditional hours Sun.* **B**

Baker & Oven   6 D4
10 Paddington St W1. 071-935 5088. *Free House*. Small colourful pub with cosy basement restaurant. Traditional roasts and mouth-watering pies from 100-year-old baker's ovens. White-washed wine bar with black beams, quarry-tiled floor and pine furnishings is *open at lunchtime only. Closed Sat lunchtime and all day Sun.* **B L D** (Reserve)

The Beehive   6 B4
7 Homer St W1. 071-262 6581. *Whitbread*. Small friendly local

in an area that, up until about 100 years ago, was an apiary producing honey for the breakfast tables of London, hence the pub's name. Country pub atmosphere. **B**

🍺 Coach Makers Arms   6 D5
88 Marylebone Lane W1. 071-935 9311. *Charrington.* A village pub in the centre of London, well-known for its good food. Decorated with coaching and racing prints. Large room with bar upstairs. *Closed Sun.* **B**

🍺 Dover Castle   6 D4
43 Weymouth Mews W1. 071-636 9248. *Courage.* Originally an 18th-century pub made up of separate bars. They have now all been run into one but there are still strip mirrors in the ceiling from where the coachmen, drinking in one bar, could note when their employers finished their drinks, in another bar, and beat them to the coach door. Good food served in a separate eating room. Seats outside in the mews in fine weather. *Closed Sat & Sun.* **B**

🍺 Duke of York   6 B5
45 Harrowby St W1. 071-723 2914. *Charrington.* A rugby, cricket and hockey enthusiasts' pub, proud of its collection of ceramic figures of famous sporting personalities. Tables and chairs outside among the potted plants and window boxes. *Open to 23.00 Sun.* **B** *(not lunchtime)*

🍺 The George   6 E4
55 Great Portland St W1. 071-636 0863. *Greene King.* Popular Edwardian pub, always packed with employees from the nearby BBC. Outside is decorated with hanging baskets and coach lamps. Inside there are two bars – the George and the Glue Pot. The latter was so christened by Sir Henry Wood when he was conducting at Queen's Hall and his orchestra were frequently late back from visits to this, their local. *Open to 18.00 Sat. Closed Sun lunchtime.* **B**

🍺 Marquis of Anglesea   6 B4
77 Ashmill St NW1. 071-723 7873. *Charles Wells.* Small pub with a very pleasant atmosphere. It was originally divided into three bars but now has a large horseshoe bar with original gaslight fittings. Pool table. **B** *(not Sun)*

🍺 Pontefract Castle   6 D5
71-73 Wigmore St W1. 071-486 3551. *Charrington.* Attractive modern pub serving several real ales and five malt whiskies.

Pontefract Castle

Inside is decorated with antiques, seachests, pictures from Pears Annual and Victorian porn. **B** *(not Sun)*

Worcester Arms 6 C5
89 George St W1. 071-935 6050. *Free House.* Small, traditional pub with intimate mock-Regency decor. Four real ales and a 'guest beer of the week'. Very much a drinker's pub with a loyal local following. *Open traditional hours Sat.* **B** *(not Sat & Sun)*

REGENT'S PARK & ST JOHN'S WOOD

NW1, NW8. Between St John's Wood and Marylebone stations and including Regent's Park itself and Primrose Hill.

Regent's Park is one of London's most satisfying open spaces. It was designed for the Prince Regent at the beginning of the 19th century by John Nash. It has a cricket ground, a bandstand, a lake and an open-air theatre, as well as lovely gardens and tree-lined walks. It is also the home of London Zoo.

North of the Park is Primrose Hill with its lovely views, and to the west is St John's Wood, probably best-known for Lord's Cricket Ground, home of the Marylebone Cricket Club, the premier cricket club in Britain.

Tubes: Marylebone, Baker Street, Regent's Park, Great Portland Street, St John's Wood.

The Clifton   1 F5
96 Clifton Hill NW8. 071-624 5233. *Taylor Walker*. Discreetly sheltered in a leafy street, it was in the snug here that Edward VII and Lillie Langtry used to rendezvous. There are three drinking areas served by an impressive carved oak bar, decorated with prints of Lillie and the wayward King. Open fireplaces give the pub a homely feel. Delightful patio forecourt for al fresco drinking and a glass conservatory at the back where you can enjoy good, varied pub food. *Open all day Sat.* **B**

🍺 Crockers   6 A3
24 Aberdeen Pl NW8. 071-286 6608. *Free House*. Known as Crocker's Folly until 1983 because its founder, Frank Crocker, built it on the mistaken assumption that Marylebone Station, with all its thirsty travellers, was about to be built nearby. It wasn't, and he was ruined. His ghost is said to haunt the pub, still waiting for the trains to stop across the road. The main bar is resplendent in marble. The ornate ceiling is also remarkable. Live music on *Wed & Sun.* Traditional English food available all day. **B L D**

🍺 The Lansdowne   2 D4
90 Gloucester Ave NW1. 071-483 0409. *Charrington*. In a quiet, residential corner behind Primrose Hill, this modern pub has a very comfortable feel. Bare boards, wooden furniture, comfy sofas and lots of flowers. Excellent food menu changes frequently. **L** *(not Mon)* **D**

🍺 Ordnance Arms   2 A5
29 Ordnance Hill NW8. 071-722 0278. *Charrington*. Built 300 years ago, in the middle of fields, as private army quarters. Houses a fascinating collection of army and cavalry memorabilia. Conservatory, garden and regular summer barbecues. The England cricket team drink here alongside well-heeled locals. **B**

🍺 Pembroke Castle   2 D4
150 Gloucester Ave NW1. 071-483 2927. *Whitbread*. Refurbished in traditional style, this cheerful pub has a welcoming local feel. Large selection of bitter and good bar food. **B**

Rossetti   2 A5
23 Queen's Grove NW8. 071-722 7141. *Fuller's*. Elegant split-level pub/trattoria named after Dante Gabriel Rossetti, the Victorian poet and painter. The pub is on the ground floor – light and airy with mirrors, plants and statues. Brasserie-style

food in the main bar; the trattoria above has a varied menu. *Open all day Fri & Sat.* **B L D** *(Reserve)*

Warrington Hotel 5 F3
93 Warrington Cres W9. 071-286 2929. *Fuller's.* No longer an hotel, but an old gin palace with fantastic art nouveau decoration. The imposing entrance is lit by ornate lamps and inside there is stained glass, chandeliers and a crescent-shaped bar with brass footrail. Beer garden at the side. Thai food served upstairs. **B L D**

CAMDEN TOWN & KENTISH TOWN

NW1, NW5. Camden Town and Kentish Town form a line from Euston Road north to Archway.

In the 18th century this was a rural area beyond London, visited by people who came on day trips to enjoy the countryside. The many inns in the area would be visited by travellers, and execution cortèges would stop here for refreshment on their way to the gallows at Tyburn. In Edwardian times horse buses would bring Londoners to Camden's many public houses to be entertained.

Very much a Bohemian area, this bustling district now has a huge range of cafés, bars, restaurants, shops and markets catering for the needs of a multiracial population. At its hub is Camden Lock which is home to the original Camden Market.

Kentish Town, Camden's residential neighbour, is quieter and more relaxed.

Tubes: Camden Town, Chalk Farm, Kentish Town.

Assembly House 2 E3
292-294 Kentish Town Rd NW5. 071-485 2031. *Truman.* An earlier inn on this site was an assembly point for travellers who would set out in convoy to outface highwaymen. Was once also an assembly point for the film crew who shot part of *The Villains,* with Richard Burton, here. Pleasant Victorian interior with lovely mirrors and interesting woodwork.

The Black Cap 2 F5
171 Camden High St NW1. 071-485 1742. *Charrington.* Built in 1776, this pub was originally a courthouse. When pronouncing a sentence of death, the judge would don a black cap, hence the name. The pub's history is illustrated

on tiles in one of the bars. Now a popular drag pub with dance floor and entertainment *six nights a week*. Quieter bar upstairs. Predominantly gay clientele. *Open to 02.00, to 22.30 Sun.*

🍺 Buck's Head   2 E5
202 Camden High St NW1. 071-284 1513. *Courage*. Ideally situated next to Camden Market, this bistro-style pub gets very busy at lunchtime. Coffee always available. Pavement seating in summer. **B**

🍺 Eliza Doolittle   6 G1
3 Ossulston St NW1. 071-387 0836. *Ind Coope*. Theme pub named after the heroine of Bernard Shaw's *Pygmalion,* who is possibly better known for her role in the musical version *My Fair Lady*. Reproduction Victoriana, with glass-shaded lights, booths and modern wood panelling. Very crowded at lunchtime. *Closed Sat & Sun*. **B**

🍺 Sir Robert Peel   2 D2
108 Malden Rd NW5. 071-485 2673. *Watneys*. Large and reliable one-bar pub next to a busy street market. A snack bar at lunchtime and a reasonable selection of wines. Garden at the back. **B** *(not eve)*

ISLINGTON

WC1, NW1, N1. Due north of the city, Islington was a fashionable place to live in the late 18th and early 19th centuries. The area began to decay a little in the early part of this century, but has become popular again in recent years and many of the attractive Georgian buildings have been restored and gentrified. The heart of Islington is Upper Street, a cosmopolitan mile of shops, cafés, pubs, wine bars and restaurants. Camden Passage, near Islington Green, is well-known for its market and antique shops.

Tubes: Angel, Highbury & Islington.

🍺 The Albion   3 D4
10 Thornhill Rd N1. 071-607 7450. *Courage*. Albion was the Celtic and then the Latin name for England. Formerly a tea house and a dairy before it became a coaching inn, this is an elegant tavern which was rebuilt after destruction in the Second World War. Situated in a winding street of fine houses and mews cottages, it has an award-winning beer

The Albion

garden with trellis work and climbing roses. Barbecues *in summer*. **B**

Camden Head 3 E5
2 Camden Walk N1. 071-359 0851. *Youngers.* Lovely Victorian pub situated by Camden Passage antique market. Beautifully etched glass, and mahogany and oak panels. Large forecourt for summertime drinking. Theakston's Best Bitter is the best-seller. **B** *(not eve)*

Compton Arms 3 E3
4 Compton Ave N1. 071-359 2645. *Greene King.* Cosy, old-fashioned cottage pub hidden in a cobbled mews. Very friendly owners and staff, so a large local following. Low ceilings, wooden settles and charming old prints of the ancient borough of 'Isledon' on the walls. Excellent range of cask beers. The back terrace is lovely in summer. **B**

The Eagle 7 F1
2 Shepherdess Walk N1. 071-253 4715. *Charrington.* Once part of the complex that included the Grecian Theatre, a pala-tial music hall. Immortalised in the Cockney song *Pop Goes the Weasel.* In the late 19th and early 20th century, workers in the clothing industry would 'pop' (pawn) their 'weasel' (a tailor's iron). It still has an old-world atmosphere with pictures of some of the best-loved music hall stars on the walls. Large beer garden. *Closed Sat & Sun.* **B**

● **Hansler Arms** 7 C2
133 King's Cross Rd WC1. 071-837 4445. *Whitbread*. One of the smallest pubs in London, named after Joseph Hansler, the first man to be knighted by Queen Victoria. This was a simple beer house until it got its full licence in 1960. Old *Punch* cartoons and Victorian prints line the walls. **B**

Hen & Chickens 3 E3
109 St Paul's Rd N1. 071-359 1030. *Charrington*. Snug and comfortable pub overlooking the chaotic Highbury Corner. An old Charrington Toby jug mirror hangs above the fireplace. Live music, mostly blues, *Mon & Thur-Sat*. Also houses the Hen & Chickens Theatre upstairs. *Open to 24.00 Mon, to 01.00 Thur-Sat*. **B**

Island Queen 3 E6
87 Noel Rd N1. 071-226 5507. *Charrington*. For those in search of a bizarre pub, this has without doubt the most outlandish decor of any pub in London. Giant, papier-mâché caricatures of politicians and famous figures are suspended from the ceiling. Upstairs restaurant, where you can eat as much as you like of a three-course set meal, is *open for dinner Fri & Sat, and for lunch Sun*. **B L D**

King's Head 3 E5
115 Upper St N1. 071-226 1916. *Taylor Walker*. This Victorian pub is home to one of London's leading fringe theatres which specialises in enterprising plays written by young writers. The theatre is at the back – you can order the set meal (traditional English menu) then stay at your table for the play. There is also live music in the bar – folk, rock and jazz from *Mon-Fri* and on *Sat eve*. Theatre performances *Tue-Sat, with a Sat matinée*. Pub licensed *to 24.00 Mon-Sat*. **D** *(Reserve)*

● **Marquess Tavern** 3 F4
32 Canonbury St N1. 071-354 2975. *Youngs*. Situated near the New River Walk, this palatial pub has an elegant atmosphere. The comfortable and plush room at the back has a high ceiling, embossed wallpaper, marble pillars, chandeliers and an open fire. There is also a small section set aside for darts players and locals who want a quiet pint. Seating outside in summer. **B** *(not Sun)*

● **Skinners Arms** 7 B2
114 Judd St WC1. 071-837 6521. *Greene King*. Named after the Worshipful Company of Skinners, the medieval Guild of fur merchants, this was once a dilapidated old house which underwent extensive renovation to make it into a small, traditional

bar. Widely used by the local town hall and railway workers. *Closed Sat & Sun.* **B** *(not Sun)*

◐ **Slug & Lettuce**   **3 E5**
1 Islington Green N1. 071-226 3864. *Courage.* Situated on Islington Green, this is a bustling popular pub with enormous windows facing out onto busy Upper Street. Scrubbed oak tables and bottle-green walls. Bistro-style home-made food. **B** *(not Sun)*

◐ **Waterside Inn**   **3 B6**
82 York Way N1. 071-837 7118. *Whitbread.* An old ware-house on the Regent's Canal which has been reconstructed as a 17th-century pub, complete with bare boards, beams and exposed brickwork. A terrace at the back overlooks Battlebridge Basin, the stretch of water which marks the boundary between Camden and Islington. Carvery on *Sun.* *Open traditional hours Sat.* **B**

HAMPSTEAD & HIGHGATE

NW3, N6. Two hilltop villages to the north of the city centre.

In the 18th century Hampstead was a country village, popular for its spring waters which were considered to have health-giving properties. By the end of the 19th century the area had become very fashionable and was the home of writers and artists.

Hampstead Heath is one of London's largest open spaces and separates Hampstead from Highgate, which began to grow at much the same time and now has the feel of a small market town.

Both areas retain their appealing village-like atmosphere and their literary and artistic connections – it is still fashionable for writers and artists of all persuasions to live here. Dick Turpin ranged over the Heath, and drank or hid in most of the local inns. To the north of the Heath stands a beautiful Georgian building, Kenwood House, with its art collection and superb grounds in which stands a domed concert platform beside a lake. On summer evenings, classical music concerts are held here.

Original London Walks run *The Old Hampstead Village Pub Walk* which explores the history of this perfectly preserved Georgian village and takes you to some of the local pubs en route. *Phone 071-624 3978 for details.*

Tubes: Golders Green, Hampstead, Belsize Park, Tufnell Park, Archway, Highgate.

🍺 The Bull
North Hill N6. 081-340 4412. *Taylor Walker.* Close to Highgate Wood, this 400-year-old inn once supplied lodgings to Hogarth, Cruikshank, Landseer and Millais. The 18th-century animal painter, George Morland, whose picture is in the bar, used to sit outside and contemplate passing coach horses. There are chairs on the front patio and paved, tree-lined gardens. Barbecues *in summer.*

🍺 Duke's Head
16 Highgate High St N6. 081-340 6688. *Charrington.* 16th-century coaching inn which still has the archway through which coaches passed to unload in the yard. Prints of the village from former days hang on the old stippled walls. Made pretty outside with flowery window boxes. **B** *(not eve)*

The Duke's Head

🍺 The Flask
77 Highgate West Hill N6. 081-340 3969. *Ind Coope.* This famous Highgate tavern should not be confused with its Hampstead namesake. Dating back to 1663, both pubs were named after the flasks which people used to buy here to fill with water at the Hampstead Wells. Dick Turpin once hid in the cellars, William Hogarth sketched drunken scenes in the bar and Karl Marx (buried in nearby Highgate Cemetery) was a regular. English restaurant. Attractive courtyard for outdoor drinking in summer. Open fire in winter. **B L** *(Reserve) (not Sat & Sun)*

Freemason's Arms 1 G1

32 Downshire Hill NW3. 071-435 4498. *Charrington.* Popular Hampstead pub which boasts of having the largest pub garden in London. It has an upper and lower terrace, a small summer-house, rustic furniture and lots of roses. Also a court for pell mell – a kind of old English skittles or lawn billiards (though now largely unused) – and an indoor skittle alley. **B**

Holly Bush 1 F1

22 Holly Mount, off Heath St NW3. 071-435 2892. *Benskins.* Picturesque rambling pub dating back to 1796. Its name comes from the old Saxon custom of hanging a bush over the pub door to indicate that fresh beer had been brewed. Rumour has it that the overthrow of Cromwell was plotted within these walls. Edwardian gas lamps and a dark and sagging ceiling. Jazz on *Sun eve*, occasional theatre. Home-cooked food. **B** *(not Sun eve)*

The Holly Bush

Horse & Groom 1 F1

68 Heath St NW3. 071-435 3140. *Youngs.* An imposing Edwardian building with a comfortable interior. Sepia pictures of Hampstead adorn the walls. Jazz venue upstairs which stages live bands. **B**

🍺 Jack Straw's Castle
North End Way NW3. 071-435 8885. *Bass.* Rebuilt in the '60s on the site of an old coaching inn which was named after one of the leaders of the Peasant Revolt of 1381. Up until the early 1800s foxes were hunted from Hampstead Heath to Hyde Park, and it was outside this pub that the hounds used to meet. Unusual weatherboard frontage and marvellous views over the Heath to the City. Courtyard with tables and chairs for outdoor drinking. **B L** *(not Sat)* **D** *(Reserve)*

Jack Straw's Castle

🍺 King of Bohemia   1 F1
10 Hampstead High St NW3. 071-435 6513. *Whitbread.* Named after Frederick V, who married the daughter of James I and later became King of Bohemia. Bow-fronted Georgian pub with a cheery and relaxing atmosphere. Prints of Hampstead adorn the walls. Good home-cooked snacks. **B**

🍺 Old Bull & Bush
North End Rd NW3. 081-455 3685. *Taylor Walker.* Attractive 17th-century building, once the country home of the painter William Hogarth, who planted the pub's famous yew trees. Concerts and sing-songs were held in the grounds of the pub and this is *the* Old Bull & Bush, made famous in the Florrie Forde song of the same name. Lots of pictures of music hall stars in the Florrie Forde Bar. Pleasant forecourt for summertime drinking. **B**

🍺 Sir Richard Steele   2 C3
97 Haverstock Hill NW3. 071-722 1003. *Free House.* Named after the Irish dramatist and essayist, whose image is etched into a stained-glass window. Traditional atmosphere with a high percentage of regulars, many of them actors. Bar snacks limited to sandwiches. Directors, Flowers. **B** *(not Sun)*

Spaniard's Inn

Spaniard's Rd NW3. 081-455 3276. *Charrington*. Renowned 16th-century inn, once the residence of the Spanish Ambassador to the court of James I. The poets Shelley, Keats and Byron drank here, as did Charles Dickens. The garden of the inn was the scene of the arrest of Mrs Bardell in the *Pickwick Papers*. Dick Turpin stayed here when he was riding and robbing with Tom King. His pistols are on display, as well as a musket ball he fired while waylaying the Royal Mail coach. Interior has beamed ceilings and cosy nooks with oak settles. Delightful rose garden complete with aviary. Home-cooked food. **B**

Swiss Cottage   1 G4

98 Finchley Rd NW3. 071-722 3487. *Samuel Smith*. Huge, rambling pub after which the area was named. The exterior is a parody of a Swiss chalet and there is a preservation order on its appearance. Inside there are two large ground floor bars serving real ale and bar snacks, a tap room and a pool room with six tables. **B**

The Victoria

28 North Hill N6. 081-340 4609. *Whitbread*. Originally a beer shop and grocers, this turn-of-the-century pub offers six real ales, a beer garden at the back and live jazz on *Sun night*. Has a strong local following. **B**

Wells Tavern   1 G1

30 Well Walk NW3. 071-794 2806. *Whitbread*. Built in the 1830s close to the original source of the health-giving spring waters. Constable and Keats lived nearby. **B** *(not Sun)*

KILBURN, WEST HAMPSTEAD & CRICKLEWOOD

NW2, NW6. North west of the city, the main roads through this area are Kilburn High Road and Cricklewood Broadway. West Hampstead is separated from Hampstead by Finchley Road.

Kilburn has been a major thoroughfare since Roman times. In medieval times Kilburn Priory was established and by the early 18th century Kilburn Wells drew Londoners to the fashionable spa. Not a particularly fashionable area today, though parts of West Hampstead still retain some village charm. Cricklewood was once a small village on the Edgware Road and is now mainly residential with some light industry. The many pubs in the area reflect the large Irish population.

Tubes: West Hampstead, Kilburn.

Biddy Mulligan's   **1 D5**
205 Kilburn High Rd NW6. 071-624 2066. *Courage*. A mainly
Irish clientele gather in this charming, cosy pub. Irish cooking
and live music *every night. Open to 24.00.* **B**

● **Cricklewood Hotel**   **1 A1**
301 Cricklewood Bdwy NW2. 081-450 7469. *Taylor Walker*.
Fine exterior and interesting original features in the large
lounge bar. Function room has occasional live music.

● **Prince of Wales**   **1 D1**
37 Fortune Green Rd NW6. 071-435 0653. *Courage*. Modern, split-
level bar. Upstairs, a spacious glass-roofed conservatory overlooks
the sheltered garden, where barbecues are cooked in fine weather.
Attracts a young crowd with its two pool tables. **B** *(not eve)*

Production Village   **1 A1**
108 Cricklewood Lane NW2. 081-450 9361. *Charrington*.
Production Village used to be a film studio and although films
are still occasionally made here, it now houses a pub/restaurant
and fringe theatre. The Magic Hour is a reconstruction of a
traditional Victorian pub, with a restaurant serving Thai food.
There is also a fringe theatre in the complex which puts on
plays every month. Weekend barbecues are held at the village
pond *in summer.* **B L D** *(Reserve Sat & Sun)*

WEST LONDON
PADDINGTON & BAYSWATER

W2, W9. Between Bayswater Road, Edgware Road and Queensway.

Both of these areas are characterised by large Victorian buildings.
Paddington is dominated by Brunel's huge railway station and
stretches north to the enchanting area on the Grand Union Canal
known as Little Venice. It is a lively area with a cosmopolitan flavour.

Bayswater is Paddington's more elegant neighbour. In the Victorian
era Bayswater's magnificent terraces and squares would have been
lined with large, fashionable residences. Nowadays, these are
cheap hotels and bedsits, so the area tends to attract a transient
crowd. Queensway is a busy thoroughfare, with Whiteley's shop-
ping centre at one end, and small restaurants, pâtisseries and shops
stretching all the way up to Bayswater Road which runs alongside
Kensington Gardens and Hyde Park. On *Sun* the park railings are
hung with the paintings of amateur artists hoping to attract buyers.
At the corner of the park, near Marble Arch, controversial views are
voiced and argued with at Speakers' Corner.

Tubes: Bayswater, Queensway, Lancaster Gate, Paddington,
Edgware Road.

Archery Tavern 5 G6
4 Bathurst St W2. 071-402 4916. *Badger*. At the beginning of the 19th century, when archery became fashionable, this tavern was frequented by members of the Royal Toxophilite Society – the archers. In fact, the tavern is built on the site of one of the first archery grounds. It is decked out with old prints and memorabilia of archers at their pursuit. *Closed Sat eve.* **B**

Black Lion 5 E6
123 Bayswater Rd W2. 071-229 0917. *Courage*. Traditional tavern popular with the locals of Bayswater. There is a wine bar, Winkles, down an alleyway at the side. There is also a side patio complete with chairs and benches, ideal for summertime drinking. **B L D**

King's Head 5 E6
33 Moscow Rd W2. 071-229 4233. *Courage*. A quiet traditional pub with loyal regulars who have formed the biggest chess club in the country. Five real ales plus guest beers. **B**

The Mitre 5 G6
24 Craven Ter W2. 071-262 5240. *Whitbread*. Victorian pub with two ground floor bars and a cellar wine bar called Moriarty's which has an appealingly creepy atmosphere, assisted by the fact that the ghost of an old coachman inhabits the part of the cellar that used to be the stables. Occasional live entertainment. **B**

Paddington Stop 5 E3
54 Formosa St W9. 071-286 6776. *Whitbread*. Modern pub in

The Paddington Stop

Little Venice, with a patio overlooking the canal. Sit outside on wooden benches and watch the barges pass by. Barbecues on fine weekends. **B**

Slug & Lettuce   5 D5
47 Hereford Rd W2. 071-229 1503. *Courage*. Big old pub with a warm and friendly atmosphere. Polished woodwork and cosy corners. Healthy food. Conservatory and enclosed gardens at the front and back. **B**

Victoria   6 B6
10a Strathearn Pl W2. 071-262 5696. *Charrington*. Victorian drinking house crammed with pictures and memorabilia of Queen Victoria, who is said to have called into the pub after the official opening of Paddington Station. The upstairs Theatre bar is a reconstruction of the bar at the old Gaiety Theatre in the Strand. Downstairs is a magnificent bar with old etched mirrors and mahogany panelling. **B**

🗩 Warwick Castle   5 F4
6 Warwick Pl W9. 071-286 9604. *Charrington*. Regency pub in Little Venice overlooking the Clifton Nurseries at the back. Wood-panelled walls covered with prints of the old canal system, a wood block floor and an open fire in winter. **B** *(not Sun eve)*

HOLLAND PARK & NOTTING HILL

W8, W11, W14. Bordered by Westbourne Grove, Holland Road, Kensington High Street and Kensington Gardens.

A fascinating stretch of West London, Notting Hill has a cosmopolitan feel, with a strong West Indian bias. Every *Aug* bank holiday the streets come alive as the Notting Hill Carnival bursts into action. Portobello Road, home of the famous antique market, runs from Notting Hill Gate to North Kensington. At the northern end of Portobello Road are a number of contemporary art galleries.

Holland Park is a genteel, residential area dominated by the beautiful Victorian park. Holland House, a Jacobean mansion built circa 1606, is situated in the centre of the park. There is also an open-air theatre in summer.

Tubes: High Street Kensington, Notting Hill Gate, Westbourne Park, Ladbroke Grove, Holland Park.

The Academy   9 B2
Princedale Rd W11. 071-221 0248. *Free House*. A modern pub situated in a pleasant, quiet street off leafy Holland Park

Avenue. Old-fashioned interior and plant-filled terrace at the side. Popular with local residents. **B**

Blenheim Arms 5 B5
Blenheim Cres W11. 071-727 8795. *Whitbread.* Friendly pub near the Portobello Road market. Particularly busy at *Sat lunchtime* with stall owners and tourists. Flowers Original. **B** *(not Sun)*

Duke of Clarence 9 B2
203 Holland Park Ave W11. 071-603 5431. *Charrington.* A 400-year-old pub, rebuilt in 1939 with a medieval-style interior and a Victorian bar. Has a beautiful flagged courtyard with its own conservatory bar. Barbecues *in summer. Open all day Fri & Sat.* **B**

Duke of Norfolk 5 D5
202 Westbourne Grove W11. 071-229 3551. *Watneys.* Rather traditional pub, with a stag's head and old prints on the walls. Popular with tourists and antique dealers. *Open all day Fri & Sat.* **B**

Finch's (Duke of Wellington) 5 C5
179 Portobello Rd W11. 071-727 6727. *Free House.* Cheerful pub with trompe l'oeil windows painted on the outside. Wood-panelled bar. In the heart of Portobello Road market so people tend to gravitate outside to drink. **B** *(not eve)*

Ladbroke Arms 9 C2
54 Ladbroke Rd W11. 071-727 6648. *Courage.* 18th-century pub won by Lord Ladbroke in payment of a gambling debt. Very attractive surroundings; floral arrangements and wooden bench seating in the forecourt make it a lovely place for a quiet drink. *Open all day Sat.* **B**

KENSINGTON & EARL'S COURT

SW5, W8, W14. A huge area bordered by the Thames, Warwick Road, Holland Park Avenue and Kensington Gardens.

Kensington is London's royal borough, elevated to that status in 1689 when William III established Kensington Palace by commissioning Sir Christopher Wren to rebuild an existing house. It stands at one end of the lovely Kensington Gardens which, together with the adjoining Hyde Park, forms the largest open space in central London – 650 acres. Kensington High Street is famous for its smart shops and department stores.

Earl's Court is, for many people, synonymous with exhibitions. The huge Exhibition Hall stands opposite the tube station, and only a stone's throw away stands Olympia. Between them they house Crufts Dog Show, the Royal Tournament, the Ideal Home Exhibition and other equally diverse spectacles. Earl's Court itself is a cosmopolitan area which for many years has attracted expatriate Australians, earning it the nickname of Kangaroo Valley.

Tubes: Earl's Court, West Brompton, West Kensington, Baron's Court, Kensington (Olympia), High Street Kensington.

🍺 Baron's Court Tavern   13 B1

Comeragh Rd W14. 071-385 4064. *Courage*. The closest pub to Queen's Tennis Club which hosts the pre-Wimbledon tournament. Traditional and elegant with the Baron's Court Theatre downstairs. **B**

🍺 Britannia   9 D4

1 Allen St W8. 071-937 1864. *Youngs*. A traditional English pub with a warm and friendly atmosphere. Proud of its beer, but also of its very good buffet. Patio at the back has an ancient and well-established honeysuckle. Home-cooked food. *Open traditional hours Sat.* **B**

🍺 Churchill Arms   9 E3

119 Kensington Church St W8. 071-727 4242. *Fuller's*. Snob screens remain amidst old-fashioned and oak-wood interior. One side of the pub is given over to pictures of US Presidents, the other to English Prime Ministers, primarily Churchill. Glass conservatory at the back houses the landlord's collection of 1500 butterflies from all over the world. Restaurant serves authentic Thai food. **B L D**

🍺 Greyhound   9 E3

1 Kensington Sq W8. 071-937 7140. *Watneys*. This pub was destroyed in a gas explosion in 1977, but rebuilt identically in 1979. Enjoy the friendly atmosphere in the front bar, or relax quietly in the dining area at the back. Plentiful food and three real ales. **B**

🍺 Tournament   9 D6

344 Old Brompton Rd SW5. 071-370 2449. *Whitbread*. Modern pub, next door to Earl's Court Exhibition Centre, which takes its name from the annual Royal Tournament. Lounge with military pictures on the walls. Mock-Tudor games room with pool, darts and video machines. Good standard pub food. **B**

HAMMERSMITH & CHISWICK

W4, W6. Bordered by the Thames, Hammersmith Bridge Road, Hammersmith Road, North End Road to the east and Lillie Road to the south, with Chiswick to the west.

Hammersmith is an area famous for providing entertainment, with Hammersmith Palais (a dance club), Hammersmith Apollo (live music venue, formerly the Hammersmith Odeon), and the Lyric Theatre and Riverside Studios offering an exciting range of dance, drama, music and general arts facilities. The stretch of the Thames just below Hammersmith Bridge is highly attractive and has a number of rowing clubs and several pubs along the towpath.

You can walk along the river from here to Chiswick, which was a wealthy riverside village in the 18th century. Chiswick Mall has beautiful Georgian waterfront houses, and further along the river is Strand on the Green, with more delightful riverside residences and pubs. Away from the river Chiswick is also extremely attractive – here you will find the 17th-century house that belonged to Hogarth and the small-scale Palladian appeal of Chiswick House in its lovely grounds.

Tubes: District line trains west from Earl's Court, Piccadilly line, Hammersmith & City line.

Bell & Crown
13 Thames Rd W4. 081-994 4164. *Fuller's.* Pleasant riverside pub on an old pub site – as the prints on the walls testify. Has a Victorian veranda with lovely river views. Real ale on hand-pumps. **B**

Black Lion
2 South Black Lion Lane W6. 081-748 7056. *Scottish & Newcastle.* Lovely 400-year-old riverside pub which featured as The Black Swan in A.P. Herbert's *The Water Gypsies.* Traditional pub games are played here – cribbage, backgammon and chess. Prize-winning paved garden with shrubs, flowerbeds and window boxes. Skittle alley and bouncy castle. Traditional and Australian beers. **B**

Blue Anchor
13 Lower Mall W6. 081-748 5774. *Courage.* Started life as the Blew Anchor & Wash-Houses, and was first licensed under its present name in 1720. The wood-panelled bar gets very crowded but there are tables outside by the river. Directors and Best Bitter. *Open all day Fri & Sat.* **B**

Bull's Head
Strand on the Green W4. 081-994 0647. *Scottish & Newcastle*. 350-year-old waterfront tavern with exposed blackened beams and an old-world atmosphere. The history of the pub is illustrated on the walls. There is also a framed page of manuscript explaining how Cromwell was nearly caught here by the pursuing Royalists. Sheltered beer garden and terrace, popular in summer. *Open all day Sat.* **B**

City Barge
27 Strand on the Green W4. 081-994 2148. *Courage*. Along from the Bull's Head is this 16th-century Elizabethan charter inn. Originally called the Navigator's Arms, it was given its present name in the late 19th century because the Lord Mayor's barge used to be moored nearby. Low-ceilinged old bar festooned with aged china. Downstairs bar boasts an à la carte menu. You can take your drinks out onto the towpath. *Open all day Sat.* **B L**

Crown & Anchor
374 Chiswick High Rd W4. 081-995 2607. *Youngs*. There's been an inn on this site since the days when Turnham Green was the scene of a battle between the soldiers of Henry VII and the pretender to the throne. This is a real drinking pub and serves traditional home-cooked English food. **B L D**

The Dove
19 Upper Mall W6. 081-748 5405. *Fuller's*. Mellow 18th-century pub, long favoured by literary types. The delightful terrace, complete with grapevine, overlooks the river. Inside is very traditional. *Rule Britannia* was written here; its author, James Thomson, died of a fever in an upper room of the pub. Former patrons include Graham Greene and Ernest Hemingway. The tiny front snug is in the *Guinness Book of Records* for being the smallest bar room, 4'2" by 7'10". **B**

Fox & Hounds & Mawson Arms
110 Chiswick Lane South W4. 081-994 2936. *Fuller's*. A 300-year-old listed building where Alexander Pope once lived, right beside Fuller's brewery. When the Mawson Arms opposite closed down, the Fox & Hounds preserved its title and became known as the 'pub with two names'. A pianist encourages a sing-along on *Sat eve. Open traditional hours Sat.* **B**

Old Ship
25 Upper Mall W6. 081-741 2886. *Courage*. This mid-

17th-century pub is the oldest in Hammersmith. It has been warmly refurbished, with nautical decor as the theme. Lovely terrace overlooking the Thames. In winter, a roaring fire is the major feature. A la carte restaurant. Also bistro dishes. **B L D**

Packhorse & Talbot

145 Chiswick High Rd W4. 081-994 0360. *Scottish & Newcastle.* On a road that was once one of the major routes to the capital, this pub is named after the breed of German dog which used to guard the packhorses on their way to London. Traditional beamed interior full of bric-à-brac and photographs relating to the area. Excellent choice of beers: John Smith, Webster's, Directors, Ruddles Best and Ruddles County. Morning tea and coffee. Disco *Thur & Sun.* Comedy club *Thur.* **B L D**

Queen's Head

9 A5

Brook Green W6. 071-603 3174. *Courage.* A 300-year-old wayside inn where Dick Turpin is said to have hidden on occasion. Beer garden at the back and public tennis courts at the front. Excellent home-made buffet. **B L D**

The Queen's Head

The Rutland

Lower Mall W6. 081-748 5586. *Scottish & Newcastle.* Originally built in 1849, this is another pub on the Lower Mall towpath. Excellent views of Hammersmith Bridge and the river from outside tables. Jazz night on *Wed*. Separate restaurant. Barbecues *in summer*. *Open all day Sun in summer*. **B L D**

🍺 Thatched House

115 Dalling Rd W6. 081-748 6174. *Youngs*. Thatched no more – though it used to be in the days before the buildings opposite replaced the old orchard. Recently refurbished but it has retained its traditional feel and is much loved by its regulars. **B** *(not Sun)*

EALING & ACTON

W3, W5, W13. Continuing west from Chiswick, the suburbs of Ealing and Acton are a complete mixture of tree-lined residential streets and suburban shops.

Tubes: Central, District and Piccadilly lines to Ealing and Acton stations.

The Drayton Court

🍺 Drayton Court

2 The Avenue, off Drayton Green Rd W13. 081-997 1019. *Fuller's*. Known locally as Dracula's Castle because of its extravagantly turreted outline. Large lounge bar and conservatory at the back overlooking the garden. Ealing Comedy Club on *Sun night*. **B**

Fox & Goose
Hanger Lane W5. 081-997 2441. *Fuller's*. This is a large and traditional pub, usually packed. Oak-panelling, plants and a pretty garden. Home-cooked bar food. **B**

Haven Arms
Haven Lane W5. 081-997 0378. *Courage*. 19th-century oak-beamed country pub which was used as a courthouse in its early days. Big old picture painted on the chimney breast shows a murderer flanked by two Peelers. Pretty award-winning beer garden. **B**

King's Head
214 High St W3. 081-992 0282. *Fuller's*. Large yet intimate pub, with pictures on all the walls. Has a resident parrot, Jasper, who is quite happy to talk to the customers. Good bar meals. Function room available. *Open traditional hours Sat*. **B**

New Inn
62 St Mary's Rd W5. 081-840 4179. *Courage*. Traditional old-world pub with brick walls, wooden rafters and old fireplaces. A good selection of real ales: Best Bitter, Directors and John Smith. At the back is a huge secluded beer garden and open courtyard. Wholesome English food. **B**

North Star
43 Ealing Broadway W5. 081-567 4848. *Taylor Walker*. Named after the early steam engine, the North Star. Three bars; the front bar has a juke box and a young crowd. The middle bar serves food, ranging from roast dinners to a ploughman's; on *Sun* the odd dish of cockles is served. The small end bar, called the VIP lounge, is where locals go for a quiet read of the paper and a Scotch. **B**

Red Lion & Pineapple
281 Acton High St W3. 081-992 0465. *Fuller's*. Huge public bar with pool table. The garden bar has the greater part of a tree wedged between floor and ceiling and opens out onto a real garden. The saloon bar leads into a small snug and a restaurant which serves English food. **B L D**

Rose & Crown
Church Pl, St Mary's Rd W5. 081-567 2811. *Fuller's*. This typical 1920s pub is a friendly place where locals come to enjoy a good range of bar food and real ales. Large beer garden. *Open all day Fri*. **B**

EAST LONDON
THE CITY

EC1, EC2, EC3, EC4. The 'square mile' of the City is the oldest part of London, the seed from which all the rest grew. It is built on two hills, Ludgate Hill and Cornhill, and the remains of the Roman wall which once surrounded it are still in evidence. Tiny alleyways, old churchyards and taverns which survived the Great Fire of 1666 are dwarfed by modern buildings, and the major developments in London's Docklands have changed the face of the waterfront to the east of the City. In the very early morning the area around the great meat market at Smithfield is the centre of traditional buying and selling. A little later the ancient streets and modern buildings are full of those engaged in banking, insurance and stockbroking. Archaic pageantry still survives in the City. Each *Nov* crowds gather to watch the Lord Mayor's Show with its procession of elaborate floats accompanied by the Mayor (second only to the Sovereign within the City boundaries) in a golden coach. And all year round tourists flock to the Tower of London with its gruesome history, traditional Yeomen Warders and Ceremony of the Keys.

Busy and lively by day, the City is still quiet in the evenings and at weekends and many of its drinking establishments *close early and remain closed over Sat & Sun.*

Tubes: Chancery Lane, Blackfriars, Mansion House, Cannon Street, Monument, Tower Hill, Aldgate, Liverpool Street, Bank, Moorgate, Barbican, Farringdon, St Paul's.

Barley Mow   7 E4
50 Long Lane EC1. 071-606 6591. *Whitbread.* Built on the site of a former monastery, this 400-year-old inn is opposite Smithfield Market. Polished wood panelling, exposed beams, brass lamps, wooden bar, cast-iron tables. Four traditional ales and one cask ale. Home-made bar snacks. **B**

Bishop's Finger (The Rutland)   7 E4
9-10 West Smithfield EC1. 071-248 2341. *Shepherd Neame.* Formerly The Rutland, this pub takes its newer name from one of Shepherd Neame's popular light ales. Close to Smithfield Market, it used to be famous for its meat-porter's steak breakfast. Restaurant upstairs. *Open traditional hours Fri. Closed Sat eve & all day Sun.* **B L**

The Blackfriar   7 E6
174 Queen Victoria St EC4. 071-236 5650. *Free House.* In the shadows of Blackfriars railway bridge, this Victorian wedge-

The Blackfriar

shaped pub was built on the site of a 13th-century Dominican Priory. It has arguably one of the richest and strangest pub interiors in London. The saloon bar is an art nouveau temple of marble and bronze, with beaten bronze bas-reliefs of jolly monks singing and working. Off it, there is an even more stunning 'side chapel' with an arched mosaic ceiling, red marble columns, and more monks – this time accompanied by crouching demons, fairies and alabaster animals. Various real ales including Adnams, Bass and Tetley. Patio. *Open to 22.00. Closed Sat & Sun.* **B**

Butler's Head   7 G5
11 Telegraph St, off Moorgate EC2. 071-606 2735. *Free House.* One of the few remaining pubs to remember Dr William Butler who, although unqualified, became physician at the court of James I. His medicinal ale had the reputation of being a cure-all and the inns which sold it hung out signs bearing his picture by way of advertisement. When demand for the ale declined, most of the pubs changed their names. This one, which didn't, has a large horseshoe bar with a hearty trade; a favourite 'week-ender' for City folk on *Fri.* Real ales on tap. *Open to 21.00, to 22.00 Fri. Closed Sat & Sun.* **B L**

The Castle   7 E4
34 Cowcross St EC1. 071-253 2892. *Charrington.* The sign outside, with its castle in the background and three balls in front,

gives the clue that this is the only pub in England with a pawnbroker's licence. The oil painting over the bar depicts the granting of the licence. Cheerful pub with an original Wurlitzer jukebox. Serves Thai food at *lunchtime. Closed Sat & Sun.* **L**

🍺 City Pride   **7 D3**
28 Farringdon Lane EC1. 071-608 0615. *Fuller's.* Fine views of St Paul's Cathedral from this charming pub which is like a private house inside. Clerk's Well, which gave the area its name, is nearby, and dates back at least a thousand years. Also has a restaurant upstairs, the Hogarth Room. *Open 12.00-15.00 Sat & Sun.* **B**

🍺 The Cockpit   **7 E5**
7 St Andrew's Hill EC4. 071-248 7315. *Courage.* Built on a tri-angular site, this old house was once a cock-fighting pit. Prints on the walls and the viewing gallery remind you of those days, though cock-fighting was finally prohibited in 1849. **B**

🍺 Crown Tavern   **7 D3**
43 Clerkenwell Green EC1. 071-250 0757. *Free House.* Over 100 years old and on the site of a medieval tavern, this pub has the only snob screens in East London. A tiny and intimate snug bar under a spiral staircase leads to the first floor. The walls are decorated with old London prints and theatre playbills. *Open 12.00-18.00 Sat. Closed Sun.* **B L**

🍺 Dirty Dick's   **8 B4**
202 Bishopsgate EC2. 071-283 5888. *Free House.* The original Dirty Dick was Nathaniel Bentley who, stricken with grief when his fiancée died on the eve of their wedding, made little effort to wash either his clothes or himself for the rest of his life. Mouse skeletons, mummified cats and other detritus in the glass case in the lower bar pay homage to him. The galleried bar is a lunchtime wine bar, reached by an elegant spiral stair-case. *Open to 21.00. Closed Sat & Sun eves.* **B L** *(Reserve)*

🍺 East India Arms   **8 B6**
67 Fenchurch St EC3. 071-480 6562. *Youngs.* Small, bustling pub near the river. The East India Company coat of arms is dis-played on the wall. This area was once engaged in sea-going exports, including beer – in fact, what is now called 'bitter' was once called 'East India Pale Ale'. This is a real old drinking haunt with a warm welcome. *Open to 21.00. Closed Sat & Sun.* **B**

🍺 Hand & Shears   **7 F4**
1 Middle St, Cloth Fair EC1. 071-600 0257. *Courage.* The name comes from the nearby Cloth Fair and the pub sign bears the

emblem of the Guild of Merchant Tailors. Former customers include prisoners whose cases were heard in an upstairs room and who were allowed a drink downstairs before being taken to the gallows. Now it is a pleasant Victorian City tavern and the 'local' for St Bartholomew's Hospital – which is why the pub scenes for the film *Doctor in the House* were shot here. *Closed Sat & Sun*. **B**

Hoop & Grapes   8 C5
47 Aldgate High St EC3. 071-480 5739. *Charrington*. A restored 13th-century inn, believed to be the oldest non-ecclesiastical building in the City. It missed the Great Fire by only a few yards and is the only remaining 17th-century timber-framed structure of its kind in the City of London. It has a lug-hole (or listening tube) in its sloping floor, through which the landlord could eavesdrop or pass messages to the cellar. It also claims to have a sealed tunnel leading to the Tower of London. Food at *lunchtimes*. *Closed Sat. Open12.00-15.00 Sun*. **B**

Jamaica Wine House   8 A5
St Michael's Alley, Cornhill EC3. 071-626 9496. *Free House*. The first coffee house to be opened in London. It was destroyed in the Great Fire, rebuilt by Wren in 1668, slightly damaged by another fire in 1748 and restored in 1858. The two bars are as different as if they belonged to separate pubs. Upstairs serves wines, ports and spirits to businessmen. Downstairs has draught beer and more of a 'public bar' atmosphere. *Open to 20.00, to 21.00 Thur & Fri. Closed Sat & Sun*. **B**

Lamb Tavern   8 B5
Leadenhall Market EC3. 071-626 2454. *Youngs*. Built in 1780, rebuilt in 1881, and refurbished in 1986 without damage to its Victorian character, this pub is the centrepiece of Leadenhall Market. City gents rub shoulders with market workers here. Its upstairs bar was the first in the City to ban smoking. Mentioned in the *Pickwick Papers* and used a little more recently in the filming of the epic *Winds of War*. *Open to 21.00. Closed Sat & Sun*. **B** *(not eve)*

Magogs   7 F5
8 Russia Row, off Milk St, off Gresham St EC2. 071-606 3293. *Scottish & Newcastle*. Modern circular pub which was built to replace the old Gog & Magog, bombed in the war. Outside the front door are effigies of Gog and Magog, the legendary giants who guard the City of London. Large ground floor bar which is always crowded. Downstairs is Micawber's Wine Bar. Bass, Adnams and keg bitters. Home-cooked food. *Open to 21.30. Closed Sat & Sun*. **B**

● **Mitre Tavern, Ye Olde** 7 D4
1 Ely Ct, Ely Pl, off Charterhouse EC1. 071-405 4751. *Taylor Walker*. The tavern was first built in 1546 by the Bishops of Ely to house their servants. Although it was rebuilt in the 18th century, it has retained its charm in the two small panelled rooms. The cherry tree preserved in the courtyard was once on the boundary between Sir Christopher Hatton's lovely gardens and the Bishop of Ely's land. It is said that Elizabeth I once danced around it. *Closed Sat & Sun.* **B**

● **Old Doctor Butler's Head** 7 G5
Masons Ave, Coleman St EC2. 071-606 3504. *Whitbread*. Built on the site of the original Mason's Hall and rebuilt after the Great Fire in 1667. William Butler was a distinguished chemist upon whom was bestowed the honorary title of doctor after his ale cured an ailment afflicting James I. The pub can be found in a narrow alley of half-timbered buildings, leaning slightly inwards. There's also a restaurant on the first and second floor. *Closed Sat & Sun.* **L**

Old Doctor Butler's Head

● **Sekforde Arms** 7 E3
34 Sekforde St EC1. 071-253 3251. *Youngs*. Small and cheerful establishment named after Thomas Sekforde, a distinguished lawyer and Master of the Rolls who retired to a house in the area. Popular with local office workers. *Open traditional hours Sat. Open 12.00-15.00 Sun.* **B L D**

Ship Tavern 8 B6

27 Lime St EC3. 071-626 7569. *Courage.* A real old wood-panelled City pub, said to have been built in 1447. The name was especially apt in the 18th and 19th centuries when ship owners and master mariners made their way here from the nearby Thames. Past associations are commemorated with a ten-foot ship in a glass case on one wall, an oil painting of a ship on another, and a bar shaped like the side of a rowing boat. *Open to 22.00. Closed Sat & Sun.* **B**

Ship & Turtle 8 B5

P&O Building, Leadenhall St EC3. 071-283 5485. *Courage.* Underneath the P&O Building this wine and ale bar dispenses traditional beers by the jugful and a selection of house wines. Looks like a wine bar, with its wooden floor, Victorian mahogany and bull's eye glass, but it is more popular for its beers. *Open to 20.00. Closed Sat & Sun.* **B**

Sir Christopher Wren 7 E5

17 Paternoster Sq, off Newgate St EC4. 071-248 1708. *Scottish & Newcastle.* Interesting pub, built in the '60s when the new precinct was finished, but with genuine 17th-century fittings, including the huge fireplace in the small bar. *Open to 21.00. Open 12.00-16.00 Sat & Sun.* **B**

Smithfield Tavern 7 E4

105 Charterhouse St EC1. 071-253 5153. *Bass.* Rebuilt on an old pub site in 1857 to serve nearby Smithfield Market. Still has an early morning market licence from *06.00-09.00* when only bona fide market workers are allowed alcohol – stray tourists must make do with coffee. Piano and pool table are especially popular during the morning session. Fills up with businessmen during lunchtime. *Closed Sat & Sun.* **B**

Tiger Tavern 12 C1

1 Tower Hill EC3. 071-626 5097. *Charrington.* The original tavern was established in about 1500. When the inn was rebuilt last century, a mummified cat was discovered in a tunnel leading to the Tower of London. Apparently, when Princess Elizabeth was confined to the Tower by Queen Mary she would visit The Tiger via the tunnel to play with the cat. Restaurant *open to 18.00, to 15.00 Sun.* **B L D**

Viaduct Tavern 7 E5

126 Newgate St EC1. 071-606 8476. *Taylor Walker.* Glamorous Victorian tavern built in 1869 and named after Holborn Viaduct, the world's first flyover. Opulent interior with three

large oil paintings – one of them damaged when it was shot by a First World War soldier. It boasts a beaten-metal ceiling supported by a cast iron column, an ornate pulpit-like manager's office and gold leaf round the mirrors behind the snack bar. In stark contrast, six Newgate prison cells still stand beneath. **B**

Watling, Ye Olde   **7 F5**
29 Watling St EC4. 071-248 6235. *Charrington*. Old, oak-beamed tavern on one of the oldest roads in London. Rebuilt by Wren after the Great Fire and used as office and digs by men working on St Paul's Cathedral. Pleasant, basic bar with dark wood. Bistro upstairs serves traditional English food. *Open to 21.00. Closed Sat & Sun.* **B L**

Williamson's Tavern   **7 F5**
1-3 Grovelands Ct, Bow Lane EC4. 071-248 6280. *Free House.* Jovial tavern, approached by way of a leafy alley. Reputedly the oldest in the City (built in 1666) and said to mark its exact centre. It was the home of the Lord Mayor of London until the 18th century. Serves four real ales, varying guest beers, plus Guinness and lager on draught. In the basement is Martha's Wine Bar with an extensive choice of food and 25 wines. Small courtyard with a few tables. *Open to 20.00, to 21.00 Fri. Closed Sat & Sun.* **B**

Williamson's Tavern

DOCKLANDS

E1, E14, E16, SE16. London's Docklands, covering a total of eight and a half square miles (13.6 sq km), is several areas, each with its own character, strung out along both sides of the Thames.

On the north bank it stretches seven miles (11.2km) from Tower Bridge eastwards to Bow Creek and on the south about three miles (4.8 km) from London Bridge to Deptford.

By 1981 it was a depressing wasteland, the docks having declined over the years. Thanks to an ambitious (though controversial) regeneration programme the area has now been transformed. Gleaming office blocks and waterfront apartments have replaced disused warehouses and derelict wharves. The poverty, violence, dirt and sweated labour of the old days are difficult to conjure up now, but evocative names such as Hope Sufferance Wharf, Penang Street, Ivory House and East India Dock still impart a faintly romantic aura of exotic cargoes, faraway places and imperial glory.

The Docklands area is traditionally rich in pubs, ranging from famous old inns such as the Prospect of Whitby and the Town of Ramsgate to basic local drinking spots.

See also *Riverside pubs* section.

Tubes: Docklands Light Railway stations.

The Angel   **12 E3**
101 Bermondsey Wall East SE16. 071-237 3608. *Courage.* Delightful Thameside pub on piles, with a pillared balcony overlooking the river. Its history dates from at least the 15th century when hospitality was provided by the monks of Bermondsey. By the 18th century, it was the haunt of press gangs, smugglers and pirates. Samuel Pepys drank here, as did Captain Cook. The ghost of 'hanging' Judge Jeffries apparently walks across the balcony where, during his lifetime, he would drink a pint of ale whilst watching public executions on the north bank opposite. Excellent views upstream of Tower Bridge and the City in one direction, and downstream towards Greenwich Reach. English cuisine in the restaurant with an emphasis on fish and grills. *Open all day in summer.* **B L D**

Blacksmith's Arms
257 Rotherhithe St SE16. 071-237 1349. *Fuller's.* Pleasant wood-panelled pub with blacksmiths' tools on the walls. A cosy area at the back serves as a games room with a real fire in the evenings. Occasional live music, and a patio area at the back where they hold barbecues when the weather permits. **B**

The Caxton   **12 G1**
50 The Highway E1. 071-480 5599. *Courage.* Comfortable pub
with newspaper history on the walls – the *Chicago Daily
Tribune* and the *News Chronicle* feature. Beers include Youngs
and Webster's Yorkshire. **B L**

● Dickens Inn   **12 D2**
St Katharine's Way E1. 071-488 1226. *Courage.* Fine views of
the yacht marina and Tower Bridge from this artfully converted
18th-century spice warehouse. Exposed beams, antique furniture and a brass-topped bar. Real ale, including Dickens' own,
and food on three levels. Comedy club *Thur.* **B L D**

● Dorset Arms
379 Manchester Rd E14. 071-538 9020. *Watneys.* Smart,
modern interior in an old building that has great charm and
the feel of a family local. A grassy garden to one side and a
restaurant in the paved conservatory at the back.

Essex Arms
92 Victoria Dock Rd E16. 071-511 7061. *Courage.* Isolated
local family pub; a bit of an oasis in a Docklands desert. Small
garden. Darts and pool played regularly and a disco on *Fri
evening.*

The George
114 Glengall Grove E14. 071-987 2954. *Watneys.* Three-
bar pub built in the 1930s, opposite the London Arena, a
huge venue completed in the late '80s. Fine collection of
ship's prints. Caters for office workers at lunchtime but
reverts to a local in the evenings. A pretty beer garden at
the back and a conservatory in which is housed a fish
restaurant. **B L**

Grapes
76 Narrow St E14. 071-987 4396. *Taylor Walker.* Good views
up and down river from the veranda of this Docklands pub.
Real ale, bar snacks and a dining room specialising in fish –
soups, oysters in season, Dover sole. Reputed to be the pub
called The Six Jolly Fellowship Porters in Dickens' *Our Mutual
Friend.* **B L D** *(not Sun) (Reserve)*

The Gun
27 Coldharbour E14. 071-987 1692. *Ind Coope.* Near West
India Docks and said to have been the setting for a meeting
between Lord Nelson and Lady Hamilton. There is a public bar
and two riverside bars, with good views of an industrial part of
the Thames. **B**

Henry Addington

20-28 Mackenzie Walk, Canary Wharf E14. 071-512 9022. *Charrington*. The first pub to open at Canary Wharf, situated right on the water's edge next to the Canary Wharf Tower. It commemorates the Prime Minister of the early 19th century who opened the original West India Docks in 1802. Decorated in wood and brass to create a nautical atmosphere. Outside tables overlooking the dock. *Open to 15.00 Sat & Sun.* **B**

The House They Left Behind

27 Ropemaker's Fields, Narrow St E14. 071-5385102. *Free House*. Stands on its own, hence the name. Extremely friendly and welcoming, with a resident ginger cat, this long narrow pub is decorated with prints and riveting newspaper cuttings. Frequented by staff from *The Daily Telegraph*. Real ales. Live music *Sun night.* **B**

The House They Left Behind

The Mayflower   12 F3

117 Rotherhithe St SE16. 071-237 4088. *Greene King*. Tudor inn which was christened The Shippe but changed its name when the *Mayflower,* which set off from this part of the river, reached America. This is the only pub in England licensed to sell English and American postage stamps. International restaurant. **B L D** *(not Sun & Mon eve) (Reserve)*

📖 Old Justice
12 E3

94 Bermondsey Wall East SE16. 071-237 3452. *Charrington*. A well-hidden riverside pub with fine views looking onto Tower Bridge. Timber-panelled with dropped beams, this is a London local which would be just as at home in the heart of Surrey. **B**

Prospect of Whitby
12 F2

57 Wapping Wall E1. 071-481 1095. *Scottish & Newcastle*. Historic dockland tavern dating back to the reign of Henry VIII. Samuel Pepys and Rex Whistler drank here, as did 'hanging' Judge Jeffries, and so many thieves and smugglers that it came to be called the Devil's Tavern. Decorated with nautical souvenirs and fine pewter. Restaurant terrace overlooking the Thames. Beer garden with weeping willow. **B L** *(not Sat)* **D** *(not Sun)*

Royal Pavilion

2 Pier Rd E16. 071-476 2455. *Courage*. Large, attractive pub right on the riverside – a traditional East End family place with a separate restaurant area serving simple home-cooked meals. There's also a riverview terrace and an enclosed patio area where you can drink outside. Live music *at weekends*. **B**

📖 The Ship
12 F3

39 St Marychurch St SE16. 071-237 4103. *Youngs*. Charming family local in the appealing Rotherhithe village. Beer garden at the back. **B**

📖 Town of Ramsgate
12 D2

62 Wapping High St E1. 071-488 2685. *Charrington*. 15th-century tavern with a glamorously grisly past. The riverside garden, where children now play, was once the hanging dock for petty criminals. Secret tunnels are said to lead to the Tower of London. Wapping Old Stairs, alongside, was the scene of the capture of Captain Blood, who was making off with the Crown Jewels at the time, and the tavern itself saw the capture of the infamous 'hanging' Judge Jeffries. Good hearty hot and cold food at every session. **B**

📖 Turner's Old Star
12 E2

14 Watts St E1. 071-481 1934. *Taylor Walker*. Quiet street-corner local, so named because the painter held regular assignations here. It has antique ceiling-mounted gas heaters, still in use. **B**

📖 The Warrior
12 F4

185 Lower Rd SE16. 071-237 8902. *Charrington*. The *Warrior* was the first iron-clad battleship built for the navy at nearby

Deptford. This is a rebuilt version of an older pub which echoes the theme. The lounge bar is done out like the lower deck of a man-of-war, with port and starboard lights, nautical paintings, and portholes in the toilets. Disco *at weekends.*

Waterman's Arms

1 Glenaffric Ave E14. 071-538 0712. *Taylor Walker.* Next door to a rowing club, this pub is decked out along maritime lines, with oars and barrels in evidence and pictures of ships on the walls. **B**

White Swan & Cuckoo   12 E2

Wapping Lane E1. 071-488 3756. *Free House.* Large wood-floored, wood-panelled bar with Tiffany lamps, pictures of Thames barges on the walls and books on the mantelpiece. Comfortably crowded with locals and business people. Standard pub fare during the week, Thai food at the weekend. **B**

EAST LONDON

E1-E16. Stretching from the borders of the City eastwards, north of the river.

East London has always traditionally been associated with slums, poverty, docks, warehouses, warm-hearted Cockneys, night-time violence and vibrant street markets. These elements still exist but the horrifying bomb damage during the last war and the death of the docks inspired major redevelopments which have changed the character of the area.

St Katharine's Dock, at the west of the area, is now a marina with pubs, restaurants and smart private vessels; the old Royal Docks boast the City Airport; extensive warehouse conversions and new developments at Wapping and on the Isle of Dogs have created prestige offices and domestic apartments.

The famous Petticoat Lane Market is very lively, and many East End pubs still go in for regular spontaneous sing-songs. It is, however, true to say that, although most of the pubs in the area are friendly to locals, they are not all equally friendly to outsiders who come 'slumming it' from up West. Attitude is all-important, on both sides of the bar.

Tubes: Liverpool Street, Whitechapel, Shadwell, Stepney Green, Mile End, Bow Road, Bromley-by-Bow. Also Docklands Light Railway stations and British Rail from Liverpool Street and Fenchurch Street stations.

The Bell
8 B4

50 Middlesex St E1. 071-247 6462. *Courage.* Formerly a music hall, this is the only pub left on Petticoat Lane. It has been owned and run by the same family since 1938, and has a loyal local following. Upstairs restaurant serves modern British cuisine. *Closed all day Sat & Sun eve.* **B L D**

The Blind Beggar
8 D4

337 Whitechapel Rd E1. 071-247 6195. *Courage.* Built in 1895, this is one of East London's most famous pubs, which attracted notoriety in 1966 when Ronald Kray shot George Cornell in the saloon bar. Conservatory and garden. Real ales, bar snacks. **B**

● Duke of Edinburgh

79 Nightingale Lane E11. 081-989 0014. *Taylor Walker.* Tudor-fronted building next to Wanstead Hospital. This is a small, cosy pub with a cheerful atmosphere. Occasional traditional sing-alongs. Patio at the side. Free food at *Sun lunchtime.* **B**

Duke of Edinburgh

● Five Bells & Bladebone

27 Three Colts St E14. 071-987 2329. *Taylor Walker.* So called because of the 'five bells' which rang in the nearby docks to mark the end of the lunchtime session at *14.30*. The 'bladebone' was added because the pub was built on the site of an abbatoir and bones and razor-sharp knives turned up in the excavations. Both bell and bladebone hang above the bar. Theme of the pub is definitely docklands – a ship's wheel, boats, old tea clippers and tools from the Port of London line the walls. **B** *(not eve)*

The Gun 8 C4
54 Brushfield St E1. 071-247 7988. *Watneys*. Takes its name from this area's links with the Honorary Artillery Company who used the fields outside the City walls for artillery practice. The barracks stood on nearby Artillery Lane. A la carte restaurant, The Grenadier, upstairs. *Closed Sat & Sun.* **B L D**

Hollands 8 F5
9 Exmouth St, off Commercial Rd E1. 071-790 3057. *Youngs*. Friendly, unchanging atmosphere with original early-Victorian decor. Snob screens, a clutter of trumpets, glass and brass ornaments. Darts. **B** *(not eve)*

Lord Rodney's Head 8 D4
285 Whitechapel Rd E1. 071-247 9795. *Banks & Taylor*. Named after Admiral Lord Rodney, an 18th-century buccaneer who defeated the French in the West Indies in 1782. Noisy street market outside the pub. Opposite the London Hospital, which was made famous by the unfortunate Elephant Man, who came here looking for a cure. Live music *Mon, Thur, Sat & Sun*. Bar billiards. **B**

Marksman 8 D1
254 Hackney Rd E2. 071-739 7393. *Courage*. This is a flagship for real ale in an area renowned for serving lager. It is a small, wood-panelled pub with a distinctly military theme. Rifles hang from the ceiling and the walls are covered with military arte-facts. A spiral staircase rises majestically from the middle of the pub and a glass cupola in the ceiling makes the whole place light and airy. **B**

Prince of Wales
146 Lea Bridge Rd E5. 081-533 3463. *Youngs*. Large, lively and welcoming East End pub situated on the banks of the River Lea. There is a covered terrace area for outside drinking in fine weather, and customers sometimes arrive with their own musical instruments. The East End tradition of eating seafood is kept alive with a stall selling winkles, whelks, mussels and shrimps *on Sat & Sun*. **B**

Royal Cricketers 8 F1
211 Old Ford Rd E2. 081-980 3259. *Whitbread*. Large ground floor Victorian bar. A spiral staircase leads down to the canal-side bar with its fishing theme decor and patio. Outside seating on the patio. **B** *(not Sat & Sun)*

Ship & Blue Ball 8 C3
13 Boundary St E2. 071-729 1192. *Pitfield*. Several claims to fame in this extremely welcoming pub. The Great Train Robbery

was planned here in the '60s and in the upstairs games room is a false wall behind which the several million pounds were allegedly stashed. On a more gruesome note, in the late 19th century, one of Jack the Ripper's victims was found on the pavement outside. Excellent range of real ales. *Open traditional hours Sat.* **B**

Spotted Dog, The Old
212 Upton Lane E7. 081-472 1794. *Courage.* Handsome 17th-century inn used by city merchants during the Great Plague. Dick Turpin connections, though the decor keeps to a Tudor theme with oak beams, plaster whitewash and prints. Full of City merchants at lunchtime. Family room and garden, and a restaurant specialising in grills. **B L D** *(Reserve Sat & Sun; closed Sat L)*

Still & Star   8 C5
1 Little Somerset St, off Mansell St E1. 071-488 3761. *Charrington.* The only pub in England with this name, which possibly derives from a combination of distillation equipment (still) and the symbol of an early licensee's association (star). A cosy and comforting pub situated in 'blood alley' where Jack the Ripper struck. *Closed Sat & Sun.* **B**

Taylor's   4 E4
19 Martello St E8. 071-254 9659. *Free House.* Lively pub with a delightful view over London Fields – in fact the park runs right up to the pub walls. Minimal decor inside; bare boards, benches and pot plants. Live music *Mon, Wed, Sat & Sun.* Two beer gardens. The pub also has its own cricket team. **B**

William's   8 B4
22 Artillery Lane E1. 071-247 5163. *Whitbread.* The original William's Wine and Ale House was built in 1682 and was one of the few London taverns with a free vintners licence. It was very strictly managed – drinkers were limited to a gill of spirits or a glass of malt only, and no second drink was served unless they left the premises for half an hour after the first. These old regulations are traced in carvings around the wooden walls. *Closed Sat & Sun.* **B**

The Windmill
20 Grosvenor Park Rd E17. 081-520 5198. *Whitbread.* Pretty family local built in 1895 as a tavern and brewery. A country-cum-City pub with something for everyone. Strictly speaking there's only one bar but it's divided into little areas. There are gardens at the back and side, a forecourt with seating, and tasty bar snacks. **B**

SOUTH WEST LONDON
CHELSEA & FULHAM

SW3, SW6, SW10. Bordered by Lillie Road, Old Brompton Road, Sloane Street, Chelsea Embankment, Cheyne Walk, King's Road and New King's Road.

Chelsea started out as a fishing village, became a fashionable out-of-town riverside residence, and then an artists' colony. The King's Road was built for Charles II as a private coach route from Whitehall to Hampton Court. It is now a parade of fashionable shops and cafés.

The main thoroughfare through Fulham is the Fulham Road, parallel to King's Road, full of shops, cafés, pubs, restaurants and wine bars. Fulham Pottery, licensed in 1671, still stands, but the oldest building is Fulham Palace – once the residence of the Bishop of London, now ecclesiastical offices with its small but beautiful grounds and herb garden open to the public.

Original London Walks run *A Chelsea Pub Walk* which explores this fashionable area and takes in traditional pubs and centuries-old riverside inns along the way. *Phone 071-624 3978 for details.*

Tubes: Sloane Square, Fulham Broadway, Parsons Green.

▶ Australian   10 C5
20 Milner St SW3. 071-589 3114. *Nicholson's.* Victorian wood-panelled pub with a loyal following who come for its real ales and excellent food. Named in defiance of the Princes Cricket Club, which used to be next door but moved to Marylebone and became the Marylebone Cricket Club. **B**

▶ Bunch of Grapes   10 B4
207 Brompton Rd SW3. 071-589 4944. *Scottish & Newcastle.* Well-preserved Victorian pub with carved wooden fittings, snob screens, decorative glass and fine coloured mirrors. Popular with locals as well as tourists. Four real ales. **B**

▶ Chelsea Potter   14 B1
119 King's Rd SW3. 071-352 9479. *Courage.* Was the Commercial Hotel until 1958 when it was renamed in honour of the Chelsea Pottery. Some of the traditional Victorian interior has been retained and it has now become a trendy meeting place on the King's Road. An 'alternative' juke box plays in the bar. **B**

▶ Duke of Cumberland   13 D5
235 New King's Rd SW6. 071-736 2777. *Youngs.* Named after

the infamous fifth son of George III, this large and comfortable late Victorian pub has many original features – large mirrors and lovely tiles. Public bar has the appearance of a stable, in sandblasted brick. Summertime drinking on Parsons Green opposite. **L** *(not Sun)*

Ferret & Firkin in the Balloon up the Creek
13 F4

114 Lots Rd SW10. 071-352 6645. *Firkin Brewery.* One of the Firkin chain of pubs (see *Real ale specialists*). Has taken over from 'I am the Only Running Footman' as the pub with the longest name in London. Try Balloonastic Ale or Ferret Ale. 'Sing-along' pianist *nightly.* **B**

The Ferret & Firkin in the Balloon up the Creek

Finch's (The King's Arms)
13 F2

190 Fulham Rd SW10. 071-351 5043. *Youngs.* Fine, solid Victorian pub providing a good range of real ales. Original features include wooden screens, mirrors and tiles. An arty crowd mingles happily with business types. **B**

Front Page
14 B2

35 Old Church St SW3. 071-352 2908. *Watneys.* In an elegant part of Chelsea, this pub has a comfortable 'club room' atmosphere. Pews and benches huddle around heavy wooden tables. The present building replaced an historic pub which boasted a tea garden. Excellent bar food with lots of choice from smoked salmon to bangers and mash. *Open all day Sat.* **B**

Fulham Tap   **13 C2**
North End Rd SW6. 071-385 3847. *Charrington*. Large pub at
one end of the lively North End Road market. Decorated with
brewery bric-à-brac; in the public bar is a large advertising
mural for various brewery products. Food bar. Beer garden. **B**

Hour Glass   **10 B5**
281 Brompton Rd SW3. 071-589 9314. *Charrington*. Luxurious
little one-bar pub, pleasantly furnished with velvet seating,
white wood-panelling and open fireplaces which burn all
winter. In summer there are tables and chairs on the pavement.
Good range of food. **B**

King's Head & Eight Bells   **14 B2**
50 Cheyne Walk SW3. 071-352 1820. *Whitbread*. Has passed
its 400th birthday! Originally two pubs called the 'King's Head'
and 'Six Bells', which became the 'Eight Bells' to distinguish it
from the pub in the King's Road with the same name. The two
pubs merged in the 19th century. Decorated with pots, jugs
and prints of old Chelsea. Permanent buffet. Wethereds and
Flowers. **B**

Queen's Elm   **13 G1**
241 Fulham Rd SW3. 071-352 9157. *Courage*. So called
because Elizabeth I took shelter under a nearby elm in 1567. A
genuine pub with a strong local following. Hot and cold food
available. Traditional fish and chips a celebrated speciality. **B**

Southern Cross   **13 E4**
65 New King's Rd SW6. 071-736 2837. *Charrington*. Huge,
popular pub with wide windows looking across the road to Eel
Brook Common. Light, glittery and very pretty. Run by New
Zealanders, it is the first New Zealand 'team' pub in Britain, very
sporty and lively.

Sporting Page   **13 G2**
6 Camera Pl SW10. 071-376 3694. *Courage*. Owned by the
same people as the Front Page (see above). Big windows and
light paintwork make it a lovely airy, summery pub. Lots of
sporting decor – polo, rugby, cricket. Outside seating. Good
house wines and espresso coffee. **B**

Surprise   **14 C2**
6 Christchurch Ter, Christchurch St SW3. 071-352 4699.
Charrington. Busy, trendy pub between the Chelsea Physic
Garden and Burton's Court. Takes its name from the frigate
that carried the body of Napoleon back to Europe. Nautical
prints and paintings of old Chelsea adorn the walls. **B**

White Horse 13 D5
1 Parsons Green SW6. 071-736 2115. *Free House.* A lovely
spacious old pub right on Parsons Green. It is the only pub to
serve Traquair House Ale which is brewed by the Laird of
Traquair in a stately home on the Scottish borders. Occasional
beer festivals. Expansive terrace at the front overlooking the
green. Occasional jazz. **B L D**

PUTNEY & WIMBLEDON

SW15. Moving further south from Fulham across Putney Bridge
is Putney. Formerly a convenient and fashionable riverside
parish, there was a mass of suburban building in the 19th and
20th centuries. The Oxford and Cambridge Boat Race begins
each year at Putney Bridge. There are many pubs of historical
interest in Putney.

SW19, SW20. Wimbledon is most famous for the Lawn Tennis
Championships which are held here every summer. Wimbledon
Village has several historic pubs and nearby is Wimbledon
Common, still unenclosed and containing a restored windmill at
its centre.

SW13, SW14. This section also includes some pubs in Barnes,
Mortlake and Sheen.

Access: District line tube stations south of the river or British
Rail trains from Waterloo.

● **Bricklayer's Arms** 13 A6
32 Waterman St SW15. 081-788 1673. *Courage.* Small brick
building just off Putney Embankment, this pub is certainly full
of character. The interior is crammed with intriguing bric-à-
brac. Open fire in winter and patio for summertime drinking.
Home-cooked food. **B** *(not eve)*

● **Charlie Butler**
40 Mortlake High St SW14. 081-878 2310. *Youngs.* Named
after the man who was head horse-keeper at Youngs brewery
for over 40 years. Full of photographs of amiable dray horses.
The sporty clientele have three darts teams. Outside seating,
but the only view is of the rival brewery, Watneys! **B** *(not Sat &
Sun)*

● **Crooked Billet**
14-15 Crooked Billet, Wimbledon Common SW19. 081-946
4942. *Youngs.* A beautiful setting near the edge of Wimbledon
Common, next to another popular pub, the Hand in Hand (see
below). A lovely spot for summer drinking in particular, when

you can spill out onto a huge grassy expanse at the front. *Open all day in summer.* **B**

Dog & Fox

24 High St SW19. 081-946 6565. *Youngs.* Huge old pub in Wimbledon Village on a site occupied by an inn since Tudor times. Farmhouse furnishings and a forecourt looking onto the bustle of the village. **B**

Duke's Head   13 A6

8 Lower Richmond Rd SW15. 081-788 2552. *Youngs.* Pleasant pub at the start of the Oxford and Cambridge Boat Race. Victorian engraved glass in the airy lounge bar. Large windows overlooking the rowers on the river. **B**

Fox & Grapes

Camp Rd SW19. 081-946 5599. *Courage.* Julius Caesar camped near here – hence Camp Road and the downstairs Caesar's Bar – which is 300 years old. Rambling family pub, right near Wimbledon Common, with Dickens characters peering out from the panelling. Fresh home-cooked food served all day. **B L D**

Green Man   16 A4

Putney Heath SW15. 081-788 8096. *Youngs.* At the top of Putney Hill, this is a really lively pub, with plenty of character. Two bars, one small and intimate and usually packed with regulars, the other used for pub games like cribbage and darts. Quiz nights. Plenty of seating outside on the two walled terraces. Barbecues in the beer garden *in summer.* **B** *(not eve)*

Hand in Hand

6 Crooked Billet, Wimbledon Common SW19. 081-946 5720. *Youngs.* This pub on the southern tip of Wimbledon Common, just by a small village green, is always packed. Cottage feel inside with tiles and wooden benches in the larger, more old-fashioned half of the bar – carpets and settles round the other side. Family room. Lovely little patio in front. **B L D**

Hare & Hounds

216 Upper Richmond Rd West SW14. 081-876 4304. *Youngs.* First a courthouse, then a coaching inn, now a pleasant pub decorated with copper pans and hunting horns. Has a large garden which offers barbecues *in summer.* **B**

Maltese Cat

Aubyn Sq SW15. 081-876 7534. *Youngs.* In the suburb of

Roehampton which used to be a polo-playing area, so the pub is named after the polo pony in Kipling's well-known story. Huge garden and patio, floodlit at night, reached through French windows from the saloon. A pianist or other live music *Fri & Sat eve*. The local for the nearby hospital and college. **B** *(not Sun)*

🪶 The Plough
42 Christchurch Rd SW14. 081-876 7833. *Courage*. About 100 years ago, three Queen Anne cottages were knocked into one to make an attractive wood-beamed pub with lots of nooks and crannies; one section dates back to 1550. Very busy, mostly with regulars. **B**

🪶 Rose & Crown
55 Wimbledon High St SW19. 081-947 4713. *Youngs*. Well-restored 17th-century pub where Swinburne once drank. Popular with the Wimbledon Rugby Club and right next to Wimbledon Common. Large garden at the rear of the ivy-covered building in which there is always local carol-singing at Christmas. **B**

The Ship
10 Thames Bank SW14. 081-876 1439. *Courage*. 16th-century terraced pub in Mortlake, at the end of the line for the Oxford and Cambridge Boat Race. Sets up outside pub facilities on Boat Race Day. Traditional bar with a nautical theme – ship's wheel, ropes and appropriate prints. *Open all day in summer*. **B L**

Slug & Lettuce   16 B2
14 Putney High St SW15. 081-785 3081. *Charrington*. Imposing five-storey building right by Putney Bridge on the south side of the river. Built in 1887, its sizeable interior has been divided into smaller areas. Attracts a young crowd – very much a 'party pub'. **B**

Star & Garter   13 A6
4 Lower Richmond Rd SW15. 081-788 0345. *Courage*. Huge riverside building which is a landmark from both sides of Putney Bridge. Hearty and friendly atmosphere. Beware of parking by the river at night – spring and neap tides can bring the water lapping up to the pub's foundations and your chassis! Very good lunches, particularly on *Sun. Open all day Sat*. **B**

🪶 Sun Inn
7 Church Rd SW13. 081-876 5893. *Taylor Walker*. A bit further

The Sun Inn

along the river, at Barnes, is this attractive, rambling pub. Rebuilt in 1750 on an old pub site opposite Barnes Pond, it has a country atmosphere, with oak, brasses and cane-backed chairs. Interesting old photographs of Barnes and Mortlake. Always crowded and popular with the young. **B**

WANDSWORTH

SW18. Flanked by the River Wandle, hence the name. It was originally an industrial area and the growth in industry encouraged wealthy businessmen to build large houses near Wandsworth Common. These now attract young, successful Londoners. Well-known past residents include Daniel Defoe, Voltaire and Thackeray. Wandsworth is also home to the famous Youngs Brewery.

Access: British Rail trains from Waterloo or Victoria.

The Alma   16 E3
499 Old York Rd SW18. 081-870 2537. *Youngs.* One of the finest *fin de siècle* pubs in London which has an enormous mahogany bar around which the whole place pivots. Delightful brasserie atmosphere, the restaurant at the back serves English and French country food. Occasional jazz. **B L D**

Brewery Tap   16 E3
68 Wandsworth High St SW18. 081-870 2984. *Youngs.* The
beer has to be good in this splendid old traditional pub. It's
attached to Youngs famous brewery – with its real ale, dray
horses and geese in the backyard. Meet the Youngs Ram
and Gertie the Goat, who are tied up outside at the back
every *Sun.* **B**

The Brewery Tap

🍺 **County Arms**   16 G4
345 Trinity Rd SW18. 081-874 8532. *Youngs.* An old converted
coaching inn, all mahogany, with chandeliers and antiques.
There are four bars, one of which is non-smoking. Mainly local
customers. **B**

🍺 **The Crane**   16 E3
14 Armoury Way SW18. 081-874 2548. *Youngs.* A cottage-
style pub near the River Wandle. An old-fashioned atmosphere
with low-ceilinged bars. The restaurant upstairs is reputed to be
haunted. Beer garden at the rear. **B L D**

🍺 **The Grapes**   16 E3
39 Fairfield St SW18. 081-877 0756. *Youngs.* A lovely little
local pub packed at lunchtime with workers from the brewery
itself. In fact they can arrange visits to the brewery. Beer garden
at rear. **B** *(not Sat)*

The Nightingale   17 C5
97 Nightingale Lane SW12. 081-673 1637. *Youngs.* A good old
traditional English pub which attracts a huge local following.
The beer garden is lovely on summer evenings. *Open all day Fri
& Sat.* **B**

Park Tavern   **16 D5**
212 Merton Rd SW18. 081-874 7048. *Courage*. An enormous
pub with a fireplace so vast it becomes a seating area. A huge
Welsh dresser is stacked to the ceiling with china. Very much a
local feel. **B**

The Ship   **16 F2**
41 Jews Row SW18. 081-870 9667. *Youngs*. A hidden delight
at the rear of Wandsworth bus garage, the Ship is at its best in
summer when you can sit out on the patio overlooking the
river. It existed in the 16th century as an alehouse though the
present building is Georgian. It is a genuine local with a very
friendly atmosphere. **B**

Spread Eagle   **16 E3**
71 Wandsworth High St SW18. 081-874 1326. *Youngs*.
Opposite Youngs brewery and Wandsworth Town Hall, an
awe-inspiring pub, one of the last of the gin palaces with a
preservation order on its interior because of the engraved glass
and mahogany frames. The saloon bar has an array of old
prints and a large and sonorous Kilburn clock. Occasional jazz
piano. **B L D** (not Sat & Sun eve)

CLAPHAM

SW4. Dominated by the main road which runs from
Kennington in the east along the fringe of Clapham Common.

Clapham, which means village on the hill, dates back to the
11th century. It remained a small village until the 17th century
when it became a popular place of suburban residence. It was
once home to Samuel Pepys and Shelley. Clapham Common
(220 acres) was originally marshland but is now central to the
area. Near the common is Clapham Old Town with its quaint
streets and churches, and Clapham High Street with its many
shops and places to eat and drink.

SW9, SW12, SW16. This section also covers some pubs further
south in the residential areas of Brixton, Balham and Streatham.

Tubes: Clapham North, Clapham Common, Clapham South.
Also British Rail trains to Clapham Junction and south from
Victoria, Charing Cross and London Bridge.

● **Atlantic**   **18 D2**
389 Coldharbour Lane SW9. 071-274 2832. *Ind Coope*. When
the West Indians first came to London after the Second World
War, many of them were temporarily housed in Brixton under-

ground station and then settled nearby. This is a lively West Indian pub, housed in a listed building, with plenty of enthusiastic regulars and an electric atmosphere. Two main bars with a games room for darts, pool and dominoes. Sound system pumps reggae and soul into every corner.

Bedford   17 E6
77 Bedford Hill SW12. 081-673 1756. *Watneys.* Old and interesting building with a balconied dome at one end. Used to be a Coroner's Court and was the scene of a spectacular inquest following The Priory murder in 1876. Still haunted by one Dr James Gully, wrongly convicted in what is now the lounge. Cabaret upstairs *Fri & Sat night* and improvised comedy downstairs *Sun night.* **B** *(not eve)*

Greyhound
151 Greyhound Lane SW16. 081-677 9962. *Watneys.* A good family pub with a built-in brewery serving a fine range of ales such as Streatham Strong and Streatham Dynamite – they will even arrange a guided tour. A large conservatory with rattan blinds and cane ceiling fans. Pool tables and space games. Beer garden. **B**

Pied Bull
498 Streatham High Rd SW16. 081-764 4003. *Youngs.* A large, Victorian pub overlooking Streatham Common. The bull is a ceramic image on the outside wall. Five well-preserved period bars. Outside patio from where you can watch cricket and football matches on the common. **B**

Windmill on the Common   17 F3
(Windmill Inn, Ye Olde)
Clapham Common South Side SW4. 081-673 4578. *Youngs.* A former coaching inn, this popular and lively Victorian pub is right on the edge of Clapham Common. It dates back to 1665 when it was kept by the local miller. It has two separate patios, one decorated with plants in tubs, the other with swings, slides and roundabouts. Popular opera nights on *Mon* in a room off the main bar, where professional singers perform arias and duets. Grill Room restaurant. *Open all day Fri & Sat.* **B L D** *(not Sun eve)*

SOUTH EAST LONDON
GREENWICH & BLACKHEATH

SE3, SE10. Royal Greenwich once boasted a palace which Henry VII enjoyed and in which Henry VIII was born. It was magnificently rebuilt, principally by Sir Christopher Wren, as a Royal Naval Hospital and is now the Royal Naval College. Although it has lost its palace, Greenwich is still rich in history and full of interest and entertainment for the visitor. Reminders of its maritime history abound. Here you will find the National Maritime Museum, the world's largest on its subject, housed in the Queen's House, a Palladian masterpiece by Inigo Jones, and in two much later wings joined to the house by elegant colonnades. Here, too, is the Old Royal Observatory, where you can see the Zero Meridian from which Greenwich Meantime is calculated. The Meridian Building and Flamsteed House, with their exhibitions on navigation and time-keeping, are both open to the public. The *Cutty Sark,* one of the original tea clippers, and Sir Francis Chichester's boat, *Gipsy Moth,* are both in dry dock here and may be explored. Greenwich Theatre offers new plays and classics, often with famous names in the cast. There are classical concerts in the beautiful Wren chapel of the Royal Naval College from *Oct-Apr* and again during the Greenwich Festival in *Jun.*

Blackheath is situated on the hill behind Greenwich. It has a very long history dating back to the Romans. In later times it had a sinister reputation for highwaymen and it was not until the late 18th century, when it was developed as a residential suburb, that it was considered safe. Today, it is an appealing village with many pubs around the Heath which, not surprisingly, are very popular in summer.

Access: British Rail from Waterloo East, Charing Cross or London Bridge. By boat from Charing Cross Pier and Westminster Pier.

Cutty Sark
Ballast Quay, Lassell St SE10. 081-858 3146. *Free House.* There has been a pub on this site for over 400 years, and it is now a listed building. The present pub is Georgian and overlooks the Thames downstream from its namesake, the great tea clipper, which is in dry dock. Best approached on foot from the Royal Naval College. *Open all day in summer.* **L**

The Duke
125 Creek Rd SE8. 081-692 1081. *Whitbread.* Used to be the Duke of Marlborough but the name was truncated by common

usage. Victorian engraved glass behind the bar. Occasional live music. Beer garden at the back. Serves three real ales. **B**

Fox & Hounds
56 Royal Hill SE10. 081-692 6147. *Free House.* Small and modest pub with hunting paintings and artefacts on the walls. Extremely pleasant and amiable; attracts a generally older clientele. Beer garden. Barbecues *at weekends.* **B L D**

Hare & Billet
1a Eliot Cottages SE3. 081-852 2352. *Whitbread.* One hundred-year-old village pub, in a beautiful setting overlooking a pond right on Blackheath. Victorian wood-panelling inside, hung with old prints of Blackheath and Greenwich. **B**

Hare & Billet

King's Arms
60 King William Walk SE10. 081-858 4544. *Courage.* Large, smart and comfortable with intriguing prints of sailing ships on the walls. Eating area at the back overlooks the pleasant beer garden. **B** *(not Sun eve)*

Princess of Wales
1a Montpelier Row SE3. 081-852 6881. *Charrington.* Large pub in a lovely heathside location. Sit out the front or enjoy an excellent bar lunch inside. Popular local. **B**

Railway Tavern
16 Blackheath Village SE3. 081-318 6637. *Ind Coope.* One of

the oldest buildings in Blackheath Village, this attractively renovated pub is proud of being the fourth in Britain for the sale of Burton Ale. The light, flower-decked restaurant operates as a carvery. Morning coffee from *10.30*. **B L D** (not Sun & Tue eve)

Richard I
52 Royal Hill SE10. 081-692 2996. *Youngs*. A traditional, genuinely unspoilt pub. Regulars overflow into the beer garden at the back and out onto the front on fine days. Real ale. Barbecues in fine weather *Thur eve to Sun lunch*. **B**

Trafalgar Tavern
Park Row SE10. 081-858 2437. *Courage*. Imposing tavern on the Thames at Greenwich, near Wren's Naval College. Immortalised in Dickens' *Our Mutual Friend*. All the bars have large windows overlooking the river. Upstairs bar is decorated with Nelson memorabilia. Restaurant serving American food. **L D**

Yacht
5 Crane St SE10. 081-858 0175. *Courage*. 17th-century tavern rebuilt after Second World War bombing. The bar is decorated with nautical prints and photographs of some of the yachts which have competed for the Americas Cup. Raised terrace has excellent views of the river. At high tide the river laps against the windows. *Open all day Sat*. **B**

DULWICH

SE21. A delightful village with a charming blend of Georgian, Victorian and Edwardian houses and shops. The imposing entrance to Dulwich Park is worth viewing. Dulwich College, a famous boys' school, is in magnificent grounds next to the park. The Dulwich Picture Gallery is the oldest public art gallery in London.

Access: British Rail trains to North, East and West Dulwich from London Bridge, Charing Cross or Blackfriars.

Anerley Arms
Ridsdale Rd SE20. 081-659 5552. *Samuel Smith*. Once, the pub and station here stood entirely alone and the local Scots landowner told the Railway Company to call them 'lonely'. His accent proved too much for them and they duly christened the area 'Anerley'. So in this case the pub, with its lovely mahogany panelling, is truly the heart of the district. Real ale from the wood and home-cooked food add to its appeal. *Open all day Fri & Sat*. **B** (not eve)

Crown & Greyhound
73 Dulwich Village SE21. 081-693 2466. *Taylor Walker*. Large turn-of-the-century building in the centre of exclusive Dulwich Village. Three bars in one, divided by arches and wrought iron. Candlelit dinners in the à la carte restaurant. *Open all day Fri & Sat.* **B L D**

🕭 Old Nun's Head
15 Nunhead Green SE15. 071-639 1745. *Charrington*. On the site of a nunnery destroyed during the Reformation. The Abbess was beheaded and her head set on a stake, which is how Nunhead Green got its name. Her ghost still supposedly haunts this comfortable, wood-panelled pub. Real ale. Salads and grills are the specialities. **B** *(not Sun)*

🕭 Two Woodcocks   18 D4
45 Tulse Hill SW2. 081-244 5585. *Free House*. This was formerly a shop and the original pub from across the road was transferred here. Attracts a small, local trade. Darts, cribbage and cards. Country and western duos *at the weekend.*

OUTER LONDON
RICHMOND & KEW, SURREY

Richmond is a pleasant riverside town, named by Henry VII when he built a new palace in the early 1500s, the name deriving from his earldom at Richmond in Yorkshire. The Thames here flows between green banks and fields and it is worth visiting Richmond Hill for the view along the river. Richmond Park is the largest and wildest of the royal parks with herds of deer living wild amongst the bracken and ancient oaks. Richmond Green is surrounded by quaint little streets full of antique shops and is also home to Richmond Theatre. Several pubs overlook the Green, where cricket matches take place in summer.

Kew is best known for its famous Royal Botanic Gardens, with its beautiful trees and shrubs and glittering Victorian glasshouses full of exotic plants and ferns. The river here is appealing enough to have inspired Camille Pissarro to paint it several times.

Tubes: Kew Gardens, Richmond.

🕭 Coach & Horses
8 The Green, Kew. 081-940 1208. *Youngs*. Big, old coaching inn on Kew Green. Redecorated in suitable style with panelled walls, exposed beams, benches and wheelback chairs. Tables

and chairs on the forecourt look out over the Green. Large rose garden and patio at the back. **B L D** (not Sun eve)

Cricketers
The Green, Richmond. 081-940 4372. *Charrington*. Victorian gabled building replacing an older one which burnt down in 1844. Cricketing pictures adorn the walls at the back. Pool room upstairs. **B**

The Cricketers

Greyhound
82 The Green, Kew. 081-940 0071. *Courage*. Tiny, local pub, with a mock-Tudor exterior and an imitation old-world interior. Pictures on the walls depict the history of old Kew. **B** (not Sun eve)

Old Ship
3 King St, Richmond. 081-940 5014. *Youngs*. Built as an inn at the beginning of the 18th century then expanded to swallow up the next door greengrocer at the end of the century. Dark panelling sets off the nautical decor and brass trappings. Niches in the walls house model boats. **B**

Princes Head
28 The Green, Richmond. 081-940 1572. *Fuller's*. Overlooking

Richmond Green, the original building dates from about 1740 –
a few changes have been made but there is still a low, beamed
ceiling and wood-panelling. The older regulars still mutter
about the women of ill-repute who used to congregate in the
Ladies Bar – now amalgamated with the other small bars into a
single U-shape. **B**

🍺 Red Cow
59 Sheen Rd, Richmond. 081-940 2511. *Youngs.* This cheery,
sporty pub is very much a 'local'. The public bar has darts,
shove ha'penny and a sing-song on *Sun eve* with an Irish
band. **B**

🍺 Roebuck
130 Richmond Hill, Richmond. 081-948 2329. *Youngers.*
Named after its connections with early hunting days in
Richmond Park, this is a 300-year-old pub on the top of
Richmond Hill with magnificent views of the Thames Valley.
Decorated with prints of old Richmond. **B** *(not eve)*

Rose of York
Petersham Rd, Richmond, Surrey. 081-948 5867. *Samuel
Smith.* Used to be the Tudor Close, but its Yorkshire brewery
renamed it. Large, comfortable, L-shaped bar panelled in
English oak and decorated with reproductions of paintings by
Turner and Reynolds of the famous 'turn in the river'. Good
views of the Thames from the terrace and courtyard. Beer from
the wood and a home-cooked buffet. *Open all day in summer.*
B *(not Sun eve)*

🍺 Three Pigeons
87 Petersham Rd, Richmond, Surrey. 081-332 2633. *Courage.*
Old-fashioned riverside inn decorated with prints of riverside
scenes. Pleasant beer garden and excellent views from the
restaurant which overhangs the river. **B L D**

Waterman's Arms
12 Water Lane, Richmond, Surrey. 081-940 2893. *Youngs.* One
of the oldest pubs in Richmond, situated in a cobbled lane leading down to the river. Was once a watering hole for the watermen who trudged up Water Lane from the river. Friendly, with
a strong local following. *Open all day Sat.* **B**

🍺 White Cross
Water Lane, Richmond, Surrey. 081-940 0909. *Youngs.*
Traditional Victorian pub with two open fireplaces, one rather
curiously placed under a window. The garden has its own bar

and runs right down to the quayside. Gets very crowded outside in summer. **B L D** *(not Sun eve)*

White Swan
25-26 Old Palace Lane, Richmond. 081-940 0959. *Courage.* Charming rose-covered cottage built about 400 years ago. Copper pots hang from dark-beamed ceilings. A conservatory overlooks the paved, walled garden. Summer barbecues on *Tue & Thur evenings.* **B**

TWICKENHAM, MIDDLESEX

Twickenham is a pretty suburb right on the Thames. It was one of the most elegant and desirable areas in the 18th century. Eel Pie Island in the middle of the river was home to a noisy night club in the '60s which featured popular rock bands, including the Rolling Stones. It is now mainly residential. Rugby matches at Twickenham Rugby Ground attract huge crowds to the area's many pubs.

Access: British Rail trains from Waterloo.

Barmy Arms
Riverside, Twickenham. 081-892 0863. *Courage.* A friendly pub set in extremely pleasant surroundings right by the river. Built as a school in about 1400 and converted to its present use in 1729, since when nothing structural has been changed. The two bars have a nautical theme. Good snacks, roast lunches and a patio overlooking Eel Pie Island. **B L**

Eel Pie
9 Church St, Twickenham. 081-891 1717. *Free House.* A simply-furnished bar in a quiet village street. Good range of real ales – Badger Best, Ridleys and Wadworth's 6X. **B L**

Pope's Grotto
Cross Deep, Twickenham. 081-892 3050. *Youngs.* Named after the poet Alexander Pope who lived nearby, this large pub has a spacious interior and a rear patio garden for summer barbecues. Extensive menu. *Open all day Sat.* **B L D**

White Swan
Riverside, Twickenham, Middx. 081-892 2166. *Courage.* Startlingly attractive black-and-white balconied pub, right on the river's edge. Marston's, Ruddles and Palmers on the pumps. Draught Guinness. Excellent food. *Open all day in summer.* **B** *(not eve)*

HAMPTON, SURREY

Hampton is a large, charming suburb on the Thames. Its most famous edifice, Hampton Court Palace, was built in 1514 by Cardinal Wolsey and taken over by Henry VIII, who regarded it as his favourite home. It is a huge rambling red-brick palace with turrets, towers and intricate mouldings. The last sovereigns to live here were George I and George II.

There are some delightful pubs in this area, well worth hunting for.

Access: British Rail from Waterloo.

The Albion
34-36 Bridge Rd, East Molesey. 081-979 1035. *Charrington*. Only a few hundred yards from Hampton Court and the Thames is this traditional English pub. Comfortable antique furniture, open fires and prints of Albion ships through the ages. Jacobean-style restaurant. **B L D**

The Bell
8 Thames St, Hampton. 081-979 1444. *Taylor Walker*. Small, cosy pub next to the church with river views, real ales, lunchtime snacks and full *Sun* lunches. **B**

King's Arms
Lion Gate, Hampton Court Rd, Hampton. 081-977 1729. *Hall & Woodhouse*. A pub with an excellent position, standing in the shadow of the great Lion Gates entrance to Hampton Court Palace. Inside is a huge open fire, low beams and high-backed wooden settles. Good bar food and also a restaurant leading off the bar. Tables on the pavement in summer. Tea shop open *09.00-18.00*. **B L D**

SPECIAL FEATURE PUBS

RIVERSIDE PUBS

The Thames is an immensely varied river and a pub crawl along
its London banks ranges from leafy calm to haunted Dickensian
wharves. The river enters London from a green and pleasant
part of Surrey, passes through Chiswick with its moored barges
and Georgian waterfront houses, and then flows on from
Mortlake to Putney, from where the two oldest universities,
Oxford and Cambridge, commence their annual battle for rowing supremacy. At Wandsworth and Battersea it becomes
industrial on its south bank while on its north, at Chelsea, it is
literary and artistic. At Westminster it passes the Houses of
Parliament and the Abbey on one side, and the South Bank
complex on the other. Through the City and the Pool of
London, past the regenerated Docklands, it becomes glamorously creepy with a history of thieves, smugglers and fugitives
from the Tower. At Greenwich it slides past the famous
Observatory and Wren's imposing Naval College and continues
out of London by way of the Thames Flood Barrier.

All along its banks there are pubs, among them some of the
oldest in London. Many have balconies or terraces overlooking
the water; others open straight onto the towpath.

Original London Walks run an *Along the Thames Pub Walk*
which traces the history of the river, with visits to London's last
remaining galleried coaching inn and an 18th-century pub that
brews its own beer. *Phone 071-624 3978 for details.*

◖ The Anchor   11 F2
34 Park St, Bankside SE1. 071-407 1577. *Courage.* An inn with
a wealth of historical associations. The original pub on this site
was frequented by a hideous mixture of smugglers, press gangs
and warders from The Clink, a notorious prison nearby.
Shakespeare's Globe Theatre and the bear pits and brothels of
Bankside also attracted a lot of custom to the area. It was
destroyed in the fire of 1666, and the present building was
built in 1750. Dr Johnson lived here while he was compiling his
dictionary and a first edition of the famous lexicon is on display.
A maze of five small bars and two formal dining areas nestle at
various levels with exposed beams, open fires, and nooks and
crannies full of antique bric-à-brac. Excellent riverside views
from the terrace and barbecue area. **B L D** *(Reserve)*

The Angel   12 E3
101 Bermondsey Wall East SE16. 071-237 3608. *Courage.*
Delightful 15th-century pub on piles, with a pillared balcony

overlooking the river. Dates back to when hospitality was provided by the monks of Bermondsey. By the 18th century, it was the haunt of press gangs, smugglers and pirates. Samuel Pepys drank here, as did Captain Cook. The ghost of 'hanging' Judge Jeffries apparently walks across the balcony where, during his lifetime, he would drink a pint of ale whilst watching public executions on the north bank opposite. Excellent views upstream of Tower Bridge and the City in one direction, and downstream towards Greenwich Reach. English cuisine in the restaurant with an emphasis on fish and grills. *Open all day in summer.* **B L D**

Bell & Crown
13 Thames Rd W4. 081-994 4164. *Fuller's.* Pleasant riverside pub on an old pub site as the prints on the walls testify. Has a Victorian veranda with lovely river views. Real ale on handpumps. **B**

Bishop Out of Residence
2 Bishop's Hall, Thames St, Kingston, Surrey. 081-546 4965. *Youngs.* Built on the site of the home of a bishop said to have 'gone fishing' more often than he ought. Meals, snacks, real ale and a riverside terrace. **B**

Black Lion
2 South Black Lion Lane W6. 081-748 7056. *Scottish & Newcastle.* Lovely 400-year-old riverside pub which featured as The Black Swan in A.P. Herbert's *The Water Gypsies.* Traditional pub games are played here – cribbage, backgammon and chess. Prize-winning paved garden with shrubs, flowerbeds and window boxes. Skittle alley and bouncy castle. Traditional and Australian beers. **B**

Blue Anchor
13 Lower Mall W6. 081-748 5774. *Courage.* Started life as the Blew Anchor & Wash-Houses, and was first licensed under its present name in 1720. The wood-panelled bar gets very crowded but there are tables outside by the river. Directors and Best Bitter. *Open all day Fri & Sat.* **B**

Bull's Head
Strand on the Green W4. 081-994 0647. *Scottish & Newcastle.* 350-year-old waterfront tavern with rambling rooms full of old oak beams and low ceilings. The history of the pub is illustrated on the walls. There is also a framed page of manuscript explaining how Cromwell was nearly caught here by the pursuing Royalists. Sheltered beer garden and terrace, popular in summer. *Open all day Sat.* **B**

City Barge
27 Strand on the Green W4. 081-994 2148. *Courage*. Along from the Bull's Head is this 16th-century Elizabethan charter inn. Originally called the Navigator's Arms, it was given its present name in the late 19th century because the Lord Mayor's barge used to be moored nearby. Low-ceilinged old bar festooned with aged china. Notice the floodgates on the front door. Downstairs bar boasts an à la carte menu. You can take your drinks out onto the towpath. Views over to Oliver's Island, where Cromwell hid from the Cavalier Army. *Open all day Sat.* **B L**

● Crabtree   13 A3
Rainville Rd W6. 071-385 3929. *Courage*. Next door to Palace Wharf film studios, this riverside pub is full of local character. Views across the river from the garden. Traditional beers on draught. **B** *(not eve)*

Cutty Sark
Ballast Quay, Lassell St SE10. 081-858 3146. *Free House*. There has been a pub on this site for over 400 years, and it is now a listed building. The present pub is Georgian and overlooks the Thames downstream from its namesake, the great tea clipper, which is in dry dock. Best approached on foot from the Royal Naval College. *Open all day in summer.* **L**

● Dickens Inn   12 D2
St Katharine's Way E1. 071-488 1226. *Courage*. Fine views of the yacht marina at St Katharine's Dock from this converted 18th-century spice warehouse. Exposed beams, antique furniture and a brass-topped bar. Real ale, including Dickens' own, and food on three levels. **B L D**

● The Dove
19 Upper Mall W6. 081-748 5405. *Fuller's*. Mellow 18th-century pub, long favoured by literary types. The delightful terrace, complete with grapevine, overlooks the river. Inside is very traditional. *Rule Britannia* was written here; its author, James Thomson, died of a fever in an upper room of the pub. Former patrons include Graham Greene and Ernest Hemingway. The tiny front snug is in the *Guinness Book of Records* for being the smallest bar room, 4'2" by 7'10". **B**

Duke's Head   13 A6
8 Lower Richmond Rd SW15. 081-788 2552. *Youngs*. Pleasant pub at the start of the Oxford and Cambridge Boat Race.

Victorian engraved glass in the airy lounge bar. Large windows overlooking the rowers on the river. **B**

Founders Arms
11 E2

52 Hopton St, Bankside SE1. 071-928 1899. *Youngs*. A former pub of the same name was built on the site of the foundry where the bells of St Paul's were cast. This is a successful new pub with fabulous views across the river to St Paul's itself from a glass wall at the back. Salad bar and à la carte restaurant. Traditional Sunday lunch. Beer from the famous brewery up the river. **B L D** (not Sun)

The Gazebo

Riverside Walk, King's Passage, Kingston, Surrey. 081-546 4495. *Samuel Smith*. Large pub with two Edwardian gazebos. The balconied first floor offers comfortable seating and fabulous river views. Seats at the water's edge, too. Good bar lunches and Old Brewery Bitter from the wood. **B**

Grapes

76 Narrow St E14. 071-987 4396. *Taylor Walker*. Good views up and down river from the veranda of this Docklands pub. Real ale, bar snacks and a dining room specialising in fish. Reputed to be the pub called The Six Jolly Fellowship Porters in Dickens' *Our Mutual Friend*. **B L D** (not Sun) (Reserve)

The Gun

27 Coldharbour E14. 071-987 1692. *Ind Coope*. Near West India Docks and said to have been the setting for a meeting between Lord Nelson and Lady Hamilton. There is a public bar and two riverside bars, with good views of an industrial part of the Thames. **B**

London Apprentice

62 Church St, Old Isleworth, Middx. 081-560 1915. *Scottish & Newcastle*. Famous 15th-century Thameside pub which got its name in the days when the apprentices from London's docks spent their one day off a year rowing down here for a pint or two. Lovely Elizabethan and Georgian interiors, decorated with prints of Hogarth's 'Apprentices'. Views across the river to the Isleworth Eyot Bird Sanctuary. Large patio with a conservatory restaurant. **B L D** (Reserve)

The Mayflower
12 F3

117 Rotherhithe St SE16. 071-237 4088. *Greene King*. Named after the ship which carried the Pilgrim Fathers to the Americas in 1620. This is the only pub in England licensed to sell English

and American postage stamps. International restaurant. Seating outside on the jetty. **B L D** *(not Sun & Mon eve)* *(Reserve)*

🍺 Old Justice   12 E3
94 Bermondsey Wall East SE16. 071-237 3452. *Charrington.* A well-hidden riverside pub with fine views looking onto Tower Bridge. Timber-panelled with dropped beams, this is a very friendly London local. **B**

🍺 Old Ship
25 Upper Mall W6. 081-741 2886. *Courage.* This mid-17th-century pub is the oldest in Hammersmith. It has been warmly refurbished, with nautical decor as the theme. Lovely terrace overlooking the Thames. In winter, a roaring fire is the major feature. A la carte restaurant. Also bistro dishes. **B L D**

Prospect of Whitby   12 F2
57 Wapping Wall E1. 071-481 1095. *Scottish & Newcastle.* Historic dockland tavern dating back to the reign of Henry VIII. Samuel Pepys and Rex Whistler drank here, as did 'hanging' Judge Jeffries, and so many thieves and smugglers that it came to be called the Devil's Tavern. Restaurant terrace overlooks the Thames. **B L** *(not Sat)* **D** *(not Sun)*

🍺 Queen Mary   11 B2
Victoria Embankment SW1. 071-240 9404. Moored on the embankment with stunning views of the river. A huge vessel with three bars, a restaurant, a bistro, plus function rooms. **B L D**

Rivers   11 B6
35 Albert Embankment SE1. 071-735 3723. *Whitbread.* Late Victorian pub, more or less across the river from the Tate Gallery. Particularly good view from the restaurant upstairs where you can eat à la carte or from a set menu. *Closed Sat lunchtime & all day Sun.* **B L D**

Rose of York
Petersham Rd, Richmond, Surrey. 081-948 5867. *Samuel Smith.* Used to be the Tudor Close, but its Yorkshire brewery renamed it. Large, comfortable, L-shaped bar panelled in English oak and decorated with reproductions of paintings by Turner and Reynolds of the famous 'turn in the river'. Good views of the Thames from the terrace and courtyard. Beer from the wood and a home-cooked buffet. *Open all day in summer.* **B** *(not Sun eve)*

The Rutland
Lower Mall W6. 081-748 5586. *Scottish & Newcastle*. Originally built in 1849, this is another pub on the Lower Mall towpath, nestled amongst some of the river's most famous rowing clubs. Excellent views of Hammersmith Bridge and the river from outside tables. Jazz night on *Wed*. Separate restaurant. Barbecues *in summer. Open all day Sun in summer*. **B L D**

The Ship
10 Thames Bank SW14. 081-876 1439. *Courage*. 16th-century terraced pub in Mortlake, directly in line with the finish of the annual Oxford and Cambridge Boat Race. Sets up outside pub facilities on Boat Race Day. Traditional bar with a nautical theme – ship's wheel, ropes and suitable prints. *Open all day in summer*. **B L**

The Ship   16 F2
41 Jews Row SW18. 081-870 9667. *Youngs*. A hidden delight at the rear of Wandsworth bus garage, the Ship is at its best in summer when you can sit out on the patio overlooking the river. It existed in the 16th century as an alehouse though the present building is Georgian. It is a genuine local with a very friendly atmosphere. **B**

Star & Garter   13 A6
4 Lower Richmond Rd SW15. 081-788 0345. *Courage*. Huge riverside building which is a landmark from both sides of Putney Bridge. Hearty and friendly atmosphere. Beware of parking by the river at night – spring and neap tides can bring the water lapping up to the pub's foundations and your chassis! Very good lunches, particularly on *Sun*. *Open all day Sat*. **B**

PS Tattershall Castle   11 B2
Victoria Embankment WC2. *Scottish & Newcastle*. 071-839 6548. Several bars on-board London's only paddle-steamer pub, moored near Cleopatra's Needle. Restored engine room on view. Outside drinking on deck in summer. Wide range of dishes available. Barbecues on deck *in summer*. Live comedy on *Sun night*. **B D**

Three Pigeons
87 Petersham Rd, Richmond, Surrey. 081-332 2633. *Courage*. Old-fashioned riverside inn decorated with prints of riverside scenes. Pleasant beer garden and excellent views from the restaurant which overhangs the river. **B L D**

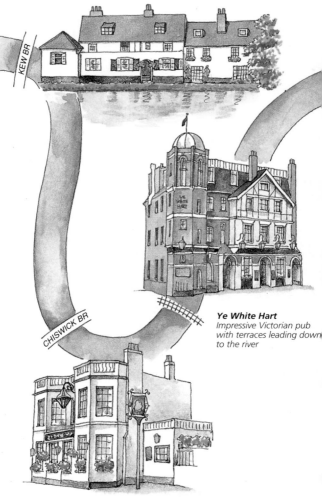

The Bull's Head
350-year-old waterfront tavern on Strand on the Green

KEW BR

CHISWICK BR

Ye White Hart
Impressive Victorian pub with terraces leading down to the river

The Ship, Thames Bank
16th-century pub in line with the finish of the Oxford and Cambridge Boat Race

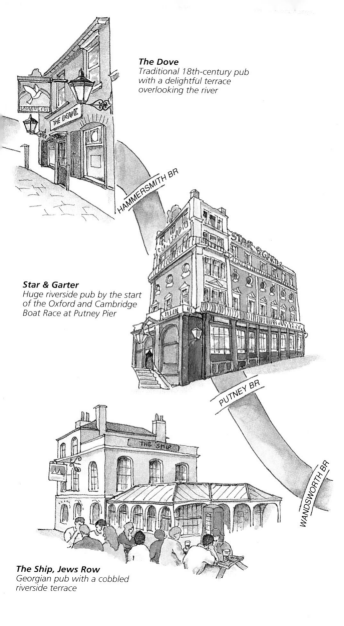

The Dove
Traditional 18th-century pub with a delightful terrace overlooking the river

HAMMERSMITH BR

Star & Garter
Huge riverside pub by the start of the Oxford and Cambridge Boat Race at Putney Pier

PUTNEY BR

WANDSWORTH BR

The Ship, Jews Row
Georgian pub with a cobbled riverside terrace

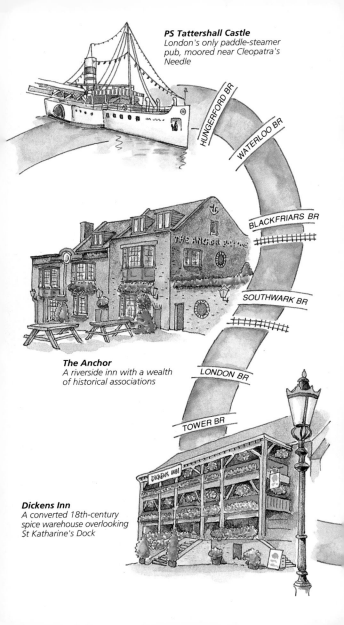

PS Tattershall Castle
London's only paddle-steamer pub, moored near Cleopatra's Needle

HUNGERFORD BR

WATERLOO BR

BLACKFRIARS BR

SOUTHWARK BR

THE ANCHOR

The Anchor
A riverside inn with a wealth of historical associations

LONDON BR

TOWER BR

DICKENS INN

Dickens Inn
A converted 18th-century spice warehouse overlooking St Katharine's Dock

Prospect of Whitby
Historic dockland tavern dating back to the reign of Henry VIII

The Mayflower
Named after the ship which carried the Pilgrim Fathers to the Americas in 1620

The Angel
A delightful 15th-century pub with a pillared balcony overlooking the river

🍺 Town of Ramsgate   12 D2
62 Wapping High St E1. 071-488 2685. *Charrington*. 15th-century tavern with a glamorously grisly past. The riverside garden, where children now play, was once the hanging dock for petty criminals. Secret tunnels are said to lead to the Tower of London. Wapping Old Stairs, alongside, was the scene of the capture of Captain Blood, who was making off with the Crown Jewels at the time, and the tavern itself saw the capture of the infamous 'hanging' Judge Jeffries. Good hearty hot and cold food at every session. **B**

Trafalgar Tavern
Park Row SE10. 081-858 2437. *Courage*. Imposing tavern on the Thames at Greenwich, near Wren's Naval College. Immortalised in Dickens' *Our Mutual Friend*. All the bars have large windows overlooking the river. Upstairs bar is decorated with Nelson memorabilia. Restaurant serving American food. **L D**

Waterman's Arms
1 Glenaffric Ave E14. 071-538 0712. *Taylor Walker*. Next door to a rowing club, this pub has been decked out along maritime lines with oars and barrels in evidence and pictures of ships on the walls. **B**

Waterman's Arms
12 Water Lane, Richmond, Surrey. 081-940 2893. *Youngs*. One of the oldest pubs in Richmond, situated in a cobbled lane leading down to the river. Was once a watering hole for the watermen who trudged up Water Lane from the river. Friendly, with a strong local following. *Open all day Sat.* **B**

🍺 White Cross
Water Lane, Richmond, Surrey. 081-940 0909. *Youngs*. Traditional Victorian pub with two open fireplaces, one rather curiously placed under a window. The garden has its own bar and runs down to the quayside. Gets very crowded in summer. **B L D** *(not Sun eve)*

White Hart, Ye
The Terrace SW13. 081-876 5177. *Youngs*. Situated on a curve in the river, this pub has an imposing Victorian exterior. Thames-side terraces at the back, from where you can get a spectacular view of the Oxford and Cambridge Boat Race. **B** *(not Sun eve)*

White Swan
25-26 Old Palace Lane, Richmond. 081-940 0959. *Courage*. Charming rose-covered cottage built about 400 years ago.

Copper pots hang from dark-beamed ceilings. A conservatory overlooks the paved, walled garden. Summer barbecues on *Tue & Thur evenings.* **B**

White Swan
Riverside, Twickenham, Middx. 081-892 2166. *Courage.* Startlingly attractive black-and-white balconied pub, right on the river's edge. Marston's, Ruddles and Palmers on the pumps. Draught Guinness. Excellent food. *Open all day in summer.* **B** (not eve)

Yacht
5 Crane St SE10. 081-858 0175. *Courage.* 17th-century tavern rebuilt after Second World War bombing. The bar is decorated with nautical prints and photographs of some of the yachts which have competed for the Americas Cup. Raised terrace has excellent views of the river. At high tide the river laps against the windows. *Open all day Sat.* **B**

OUTDOOR DRINKING

Pubs with facilities for open-air drinking – in a garden or on a terrace or patio – are obviously popular in good weather. There are many pubs with outdoor drinking facilities along the banks of the Thames. See also the *Riverside pubs* section.

Admiral Codrington   10 B5
17 Mossop St SW3. 071-581 0005. *Charrington.* This pub has a large covered garden where there are barbecues *in summer.* Also a cocktail bar in the conservatory. Named after the Admiral who led the Allied fleet which defeated the Turks at Navarino in 1827, this is an appealing wood-panelled, gas-lit pub. **B L D** (not Sun eve)

Antwerp Arms
168 Church Rd N17. 081-808 4449. *Charrington.* Given its name in the 19th century when the brewery won an award in Antwerp, this pub has a pretty paved garden, with a fishpond and a cherry tree. Part of a terrace of cottages built around 1820 next to All Hallows Church. Traditional Sunday roast a speciality. **L**

Bunch of Grapes   12 A2
2 St Thomas St SE1. 071-407 3673. *Free House.* Pleasant garden at the back which welcomes children. Hot snacks in the bar, grills in the upstairs restaurant. Youngs, Bass and Brakspears ale to drink. *Open to 20.30. Closed Sat & Sun.* **B L** (Reserve)

Canonbury Tavern

3 E3

21 Canonbury Pl N1. 071-226 1881. *Charrington*. There's been a tavern on the site since the 16th century, though this building is a mere 200 years old. Large garden with *summer* barbecues. Imaginative well-prepared food at the bar. Traditional Sunday lunch. **B L**

Crooked Billet

14-15 Crooked Billet, Wimbledon Common SW19. 081-946 4942. *Youngs*. A beautiful setting near the edge of Wimbledon Common, next to another popular pub, the Hand in Hand (see below). A lovely spot for summer drinking in particular, when you can spill out onto a huge grassy expanse at the front. *Open all day in summer.* **B**

Cross Keys

14 B2

2 Lawrence St SW3. 071-352 1893. *Courage*. Unspoilt 18th-century Chelsea local with a pretty walled garden. Exceptionally friendly staff. **B**

Duke of Clarence

9 B2

203 Holland Park Ave W11. 071-603 5431. *Charrington*. 400-year-old pub that was rebuilt in 1939 with a medieval-style interior and a Victorian bar. Beautiful flagged courtyard with

Duke of Clarence

imitation gas lamps and its own conservatory bar. Good selection of food, regular barbecues *in summer* and live music on *Sat nights. Open all day Fri & Sat.* **B**

Duke of Somerset 8 C5
14 Little Somerset St, off Mansell St E1. 071-481 0785. *Charrington.* Boasts of being the only City pub with a patio garden. Inside is a large and usually crowded bar. *Open to 21.30. Closed Sat & Sun.* **B**

🍺 Earl of Lonsdale 5 D5
277-281 Westbourne Grove W11. 071-727 6335. *Samuel Smith.* Behind the antique stalls of the Portobello Road market stands this large, comfortable mid-Victorian pub, serving Old Brewery Bitter and bar lunches. Outside, very much a town garden, with stone flags and street lamps, softened by the welcome presence of a lovely Iolanthus tree. **B**

🍺 The Flask
77 Highgate West Hill N6. 081-340 3969. *Ind Coope.* This famous Highgate tavern should not be confused with its Hampstead namesake. Dating back to 1663, both pubs were named after the flasks which people used to buy here to fill with water at the Hampstead Wells. It has an attractive courtyard for outdoor drinking in summer. **B L** *(Reserve) (not Sat & Sun)*

🍺 Freemason's Arms 1 G1
32 Downshire Hill NW3. 071-435 4498. *Charrington.* Popular Hampstead pub which boasts of having the largest pub garden in London. It has an upper and lower terrace, a small summerhouse, rustic furniture and lots of roses. Also a court for pell mell – a kind of old English skittles or lawn billiards (though now largely unused) – and an indoor skittle alley. **B**

🍺 Green Man 16 A4
Putney Heath SW15. 081-788 8096. *Youngs.* At the top of Putney Hill, this is a really lively pub, with plenty of seating outside on the two walled terraces. They also have barbecues in the beer garden *in summer.* **B** *(not eve)*

🍺 Hand in Hand
6 Crooked Billet, Wimbledon Common SW19. 081-946 5720. *Youngs.* This pub is on the southern tip of Wimbledon Common, just by a small village green. The lovely little patio at the front is always packed in summer. **B L D**

🍺 Hare & Hounds
216 Upper Richmond Rd West SW14. 081-876 4304. *Youngs.*

First a courthouse, then a coaching inn, now a pleasant pub decorated with copper pans and hunting horns. Has a large garden which has barbecues *in summer*. **B**

🍺 **Jack Straw's Castle**
North End Way NW3. 071-435 8885. *Bass*. Rebuilt in the '60s on the site of an old coaching inn, this pub has an unusual weatherboard frontage and marvellous views over the Heath from courtyard tables. **B L** *(not Sat)* **D** *(Reserve)*

Jack Straw's Castle

Ladbroke Arms   **9 C2**
54 Ladbroke Rd W11. 071-727 6648. *Courage*. Charming 18th-century pub won by Lord Ladbroke in payment of a gambling debt. Arresting floral arrangements and wooden bench seating in the pretty forecourt, which has won prizes from both brewery and council. *Open all day Sat*. **B**

🍺 **The Mudlark**   **11 G2**
Montague Close SE1. 071-403 1517. *Charrington*. The mud-larks of Dickensian London were pathetic waifs who scavenged for coins and other treasures at the river's edge. The pub which bears their name has a patio garden overlooking the 'piazza' of the next door local development. *Closed Sat & Sun*. **B**

🍺 **Old Bull & Bush**
North End Rd NW3. 081-455 3685. *Taylor Walker*. Attractive 17th-century building, once the country home of the painter William Hogarth, who planted the pub's famous yew trees. This is *the* Old Bull & Bush, made famous in the Florrie Forde song of the same name. It has a pleasant forecourt for summertime drinking. **B**

Phene Arms   14 B2
9 Phene St SW3. 071-352 3294. *Courage.* Named after Dr Phene, the first man to plant trees in cities. Appropriately enough, this small cul-de-sac pub is almost hidden by trees. Pleasant patio for summertime drinking. *Open all day Sat.* **B L D**

Railway Bell
14 Cawnpore St SE19. 081-670 2844. *Youngs.* Attractive, well-cared-for walled garden with two rows of umbrella-shaded tables. Inside, railway pictures line the walls of the long bar. **B**

The Raj   9 C2
40 Holland Park Ave W11. 071-727 6332. *Courage.* Victorian pub redecorated in carefully researched reproduction British Raj style. At the back is a paved garden with a gazebo, and in front there are benches and tables. Inside there are four pool tables and a pinball machine. **B**

Rose & Crown
55 Wimbledon High St SW19. 081-947 4713. *Youngs.* Well-restored 17th-century pub where Swinburne once drank. Popular with the Wimbledon Rugby Club and right next to Wimbledon Common. Large garden at the rear of the ivy-covered building in which there is always local carol-singing at Christmas. **B**

Scarsdale Arms   9 D4
23a Edwardes Sq W8. 071-937 1811. *Courage.* In summer, sit out under the plane trees on the pretty terrace. Inside you sit amidst old clocks and plates, gas lamps and stuffed animals. Excellent bar food and real ales. Carol singing in late *Dec.* **B**

Sir Christopher Hatton   7 D4
Leather Lane EC1. 071-405 4226. *Charrington.* A large patio in the pedestrian precinct where a street market flourishes until early afternoon. Mock Tudor design inside. *Open to 21.30. Closed Sat & Sun.* **B**

Spaniard's Inn
Spaniard's Rd NW3. 081-455 3276. *Charrington.* Renowned 16th-century inn, once the residence of the Spanish Ambassador to the court of James I. It has a delightful rose garden complete with aviary. The garden of the inn was the scene of the arrest of Mrs Bardell in the *Pickwick Papers.* Home-cooked food. **B**

🍺 **Swan Tavern**   **6 A6**
66 Bayswater Rd W2. 071-262 5204. *Courage*. This beer garden opposite Hyde Park is illuminated from dusk on. It has become a popular rendezvous for overseas visitors. **B**

🍺 **The Victoria**
10 West Temple Sheen SW14. 081-876 4238. *Courage*. Lovely award-winning garden with a large conservatory where food is served *Tue-Sat eves & Sun lunchtime*. Friendly, comfortable local pub. **B**

White Horse   **13 D5**
1 Parsons Green SW6. 071-736 2115. *Free House*. A lovely spacious old pub with an expansive terrace at the front overlooking Parsons Green. It is the only pub to serve Traquair House Ale which is brewed by the Laird of Traquair in a stately home on the Scottish borders. Occasional beer festivals. **B L D**

🍺 **Windsor Castle**   **9 D2**
114 Campden Hill Rd W8. 071-727 8491. *Charrington*. Built in 1835 when it was actually possible to see Windsor Castle from here. There are three bars, with low-beamed ceilings and open fires. The large walled garden is a true sun-trap and has a bar and snack bar of its own. **B L D** *(not Sun L)*

REAL ALE SPECIALISTS

Real ale continues to mature in its cask in the pub cellar, and has to be pumped to the bar by a beer engine. Keg beer, by contrast, is filtered and pasteurised before it leaves the brewery and is brought to the bar by means of carbon dioxide pressure which makes it unnaturally fizzy. Real ale only lasts for a few days and must be well cared for or it will 'go off'. Keg beer keeps for months and doesn't undergo any change. All of this adds up to the fact that keg beer gives the publican an easier life, which is why traditional or 'real' ale began to vanish and the pubs which served it became rarities.

Now, thanks to the determination and tireless vigilance of the Campaign for Real Ale (CAMRA), the majority of London's pubs serve at least one real ale and a significant number can offer a choice. This happy situation means that a section entitled Real Ale Pubs would have to include virtually every pub in this guide. However, there are real ale pubs which have a special appeal to enthusiasts. These are the ones which serve several different ales, and change stock frequently, so that a regular visitor can work through a great many of Britain's varied brews without travelling the country.

Another welcome development has been the spread of pubs which brew beer on the premises; this is in fact a reversion to the practice of the middle ages, when landlord and brewer tended to be the same person. It is sometimes possible to watch part of the brewing process in these home-brew pubs. Two, three or four ales are generally produced, and there is almost always one extra-strong beer which should be approached with caution by all but the most seasoned drinkers.

The Beer Shop 8 B2
8 Pitfield St N1. 071-739 3701. Home of the Pitfield Brewery, Britain's first off licence to brew on the premises. Huge stock of bottled, canned and draught beers from breweries throughout the world. Also sells home brews produced by traditional methods, and all equipment and ingredients necessary for beer-making. *Open 11.00-19.00 Mon-Fri; 10.00-16.00 Sat.*

Bricklayer's Arms 8 B3
63 Charlotte Rd EC2. 071-739 5245. *Free House.* A paradise for real ale enthusiasts – more than 50 are juggled around among seven handpumps. At lunchtime it's a City pub, in the evening a traditional East End boozer. Small restaurant upstairs. *Closed Sat eve & all day Sun.* **B L**

Bridge House, Ye Olde 12 C2
Tower Bridge Rd SE1. 071-403 2276. *Free House.* An ex-warehouse which became a pub and small brewery at the beginning of the '80s. They pull pints of their own Bermondsey Bitter and of '007' for those who like something with more impact. **B**

Hole in the Wall 11 D2
5 Mepham St SE1. 071-928 6196. *Free House.* A famous real ale haunt, built into the arches by Waterloo Station, this pub never changes. Always full of real ale lovers enjoying the 12 real ales on the go – including Ruddles and Youngs. Mercy Stout from Cork is something special to try. *Open traditional hours Sat.* **B**

The Moon 7 C4
18 New North St WC1. 071-405 6723. *Free House.* Victorian pub which began life as The George & Dragon and became notorious as a meeting place for thieves and highwaymen. Taken over by the proprietor of the Sun Inn (see below), who changed the name and introduced a dozen real ales. Friendly with a strong local following. *Open all day Fri. Closed Sun eve.* **B**

Radnor Arms
9 C5

247 Warwick Rd W14. 071-603 3224. *Free House*. A small pub, but the cellars are well-stocked – Royal Oak, Everards Tiger, Adnams and two guest beers which are changed every ten days or so. There is also draught cider. *Open all day Mon, Thur & Fri*. **B**

🍺 Sun Inn
7 C3

63 Lamb's Conduit St WC1. 071-405 8278. *Clifton Inns*. Small, bustling and rumbustious with an exceptional choice of real ales. Immense old vaulted cellars spreading under the streets make it possible to store up to 70 real ales and to make 20 available at any one time, including little-known but excellent guest beers. They conduct cellar tours – phone a day in advance. Home delivery by the barrel can be arranged. **B**

Three Kings
13 C1

171 North End Rd W14. 071-603 6071. *Free House*. This was once the Nashville Rooms, known for its visiting bands and hard-wearing dancefloor. It has now been turned into an enormous temple of real ale with 18 handpumps dispensing a minimum of nine real ales, four lagers and three keg beers, not to mention a draught cider. Regulars are Flowers and Chiswick. Traditional *Sunday* lunches. **B**

🍺 Truscott Arms
5 C2

55 Shirland Rd W9. 071-286 0310. *Free House*. The promise implied in the row of ten handpumps is not an idle one – there are ten different real ales on the go at any one time. (The Truscott Ten refers not to these but to the fact that anyone who downs ten pints in one session gets his or her name in gold on a special board.) **B**

🍺 The Victoria
2 E6

2 Mornington Ter NW1. 071-387 3804. *Whitbread*. Six real ales here. The regulars are Flowers, Boddingtons and London Pride. The other three change weekly. Barbecues in the patio garden on *summer weekends*. **B**

Welch's

130 High Rd N2. 081-444 7444. *Free House*. The 12 hand-pumps pull about 100 different real ales in a year. Those which are pretty well always on are Ruddles, Wadworth's 6X, Courage Directors, Archers Headbanger and Willie Warmer (tread cautiously with the last two). There are also six lagers and 14 country wines. *Open all day Sat & Sun*.

FIRKIN PUBS

A seemingly ever-extending chain of welcoming pubs started up by a remarkable young entrepreneur, David Bruce, to revive the ancient craft of brewing on the premises. Firkin pubs are traditional in style, with wooden floors and furniture, lots of brass and glass and excellent home-cooked food. Their own beers are brewed on the premises and part of the operation can usually be glimpsed through a strategically-placed window or porthole. Most of the Firkin pubs also have guest ales on the pumps as a regular feature. (A firkin is half a kilderkin or, if you prefer, a quarter-barrel sized cask.) In Firkin pubs, puns are an essential part of the theme; look out for them on bar staff's t-shirts and on the walls.

The following is a list of Firkin Pub Breweries:

Falcon & Firkin 4 F5
360 Victoria Park Rd E9. 081-985 0693. *Firkin Brewery*. Try Falcon Ale or, for something stronger, Bruce's Hackney Bitter. This pub features a family room and a pretty beer garden. **B**

Ferret & Firkin in the 13 F4
Balloon up the Creek
114 Lots Rd SW10. 071-352 6645. *Firkin Brewery*. Has taken over from 'I am the Only Running Footman' as the pub with the longest name in London. Balloonastic Ale or Ferret Ale, draught ciders and country wines. 'Sing-along' pianist *nightly*. **B**

The Ferret & Firkin in the Balloon up the Creek

Flounder & Firkin 3 D2
54 Holloway Rd N7. 071-609 9574. *Firkin Brewery*. Fish T'Ale or Whale Ale are the ones to get hooked on here. The brewery is in the cellar and you can view it through glass-covered observation holes in the floor. Comedy venue *Wed night*. **B**

Flower & Firkin
Kew Gardens Station, Surrey. 081-332 1162. *Firkin Brewery.* Situated right on Kew Gardens station, with a light and sunny conservatory bar at the side. Live music *Fri nights.* **B**

Fox & Firkin
316 Lewisham High St SE13. 081-690 8925. *Firkin Brewery.* Live music *Wed-Sat;* guitar on *Wed & Thur eves,* piano player on *Fri & Sat eves.* Garden at the back. **B**

Friar & Firkin   6 G2
120 Euston Rd NW1. 071-387 2419. *Firkin Brewery.* Live music *Thur & Fri eves* with a late licence. Dogbolter, Friar and Confessional ales. **B**

Friesian & Firkin   17 F1
87 Rectory Grove SW4. 071-622 4666. *Firkin Brewery.* Live music *Fri & Sat eves.* Dogbolter and Udder ales. **B**

Frigate & Firkin   9 A4
24 Blythe Rd W14. 071-602 1412. *Firkin Brewery.* Live music *Fri, Sat & Sun eves.* Quiz night *Tue.* Wingspan, Frigate and Dogbolter ales. **B**

Frog & Firkin   5 C4
41 Tavistock Cres W11. 071-727 9250. *Firkin Brewery.* Interesting collection of hats on display. Try Tavistock, Bullfrog and Iron Dog ales. Garden. **B**

Fulmar & Firkin   7 B5
51 Parker St WC2. 071-405 0590. *Firkin Brewery.* The ales here are Dogbolter, Fulmar, Wingspan, Golden Glory and Firkin Mild. They have one guest ale a week, and a beer festival once a month. Alternative comedy *Sat night. Closed Sun.* **B**

Fusilier & Firkin   2 D4
7-8 Chalk Farm Rd NW1. 071-485 7858. *Firkin Brewery.* Live music on *Sat afternoons from 14.30.* Musket and Fusilier ales. **B**

Goose & Firkin   11 E4
47 Borough Rd SE1. 071-403 3590. *Firkin Brewery.* The first of the Firkin pubs. Goose, Borough Bitter, Dogbolter, and sometimes Gobstopper, are on the pumps. *Open all day Sat.* **B**

Pheasant & Firkin   7 E2
166 Goswell Rd EC1. 071-253 7429. *Firkin Brewery.* Handy for the Barbican Centre. Regulars play backgammon and cribbage at weekend lunchtimes. Pheasant and Plucker ales available, as well as the strong Dogbolter. *Open all day Sat.* **B**

Phoenix & Firkin   15 G5
Denmark Hill Railway Station, 5 Windsor Walk SE5. 071-701 8282. *Firkin Brewery.* Largest and smartest of the Firkin pubs, the 'flagship' of the group, offering all the familiar 'Rail Ales'. **B**

THEATRE PUBS

Some of the most exciting and varied fringe theatre – new plays, classics, cabaret, revues, musicals and monologues – takes place in rooms above or behind pubs where the atmosphere is friendly and relaxed.

It is wise to book in advance, and membership is nearly always necessary to enable the theatres to keep their club status. The cost is nominal, though, and you can join at the door.

For further details of performances consult *Time Out*.

Baron's Court Theatre   13 B1
Baron's Ale House, 28 Comeragh Rd W14. 071-602 0235. Exciting and innovative productions play to packed houses at this small theatre-in-the-round. Performances *Mon-Sat*.

Bush Theatre
Bush Hotel, Shepherd's Bush Green W12. 081-749 9861. Box office: 081-743 3388. The theatre, with its curtainless stage and raked seating, is above the pub. Established to attract the non-theatre-going public, its new productions often transfer to the West End. Performances *Mon-Sat*.

The Bush Theatre

DOC Theatre Club   2 F3
Duke of Cambridge, 64 Lawford Rd NW5. 071-485 4303. Stages classical and modern plays with an emphasis on European theatre. Performances *Tue- Sun*.

Duke's Head

42 The Vineyard, Richmond, Surrey. 081-948 8085. Wide range of productions, including some ex-West End shows. Performances *Tue-Sun*.

Etcetera Theatre   **2 F5**

Oxford Arms, 265 Camden High St NW1. 071-482 4857. Performances of contemporary plays, anything from comedy to tragedy. Performances *Tue-Sun*. One-off plays, music and poetry *Mon eves*.

The Finborough   **13 E1**

Finborough Arms, 118 Finborough Rd SW10. 071-373 3842. Offers new plays, some by the resident writer, though new scripts with local relevance are always considered. Performances *Mon-Sat*.

The Gate   **9 D1**

Prince Albert, 11 Pembridge Rd W11. 071-229 0706. One of the oldest of the pub theatres, specialising in world theatre. Topical satirical revue on *Fri & Sat*. Late-night cabaret on *Thur & Fri*. Performances *Mon-Sat*.

Greenwich Studio

Prince of Orange, 189 High Rd SE10. 081-858 2862. Quality productions of classics, new English and American writers and occasional cabaret. Performances *Tue-Sun*.

Hen & Chickens   **3 E3**

Hen & Chickens Pub, 109 St Paul's Rd N1. 071-704 2001. A resident company, but they also welcome regional companies bringing in plays by new writers. Performances *Tue-Sun*. Regular *Mon night* Theatresports, improvised sketches based on audience suggestions.

King's Head   **3 E5**

115 Upper St N1. 071-226 1916. Probably the best known and most widely reviewed of theatre pubs. You can order a set meal – traditional English menu – then stay at your table for the play. After the performance, there is live music – folk, rock and jazz. Performances *Tue-Sat, plus a Sat matinée*. Pub licensed *to 24.00 Mon-Sat*.

Man in the Moon   **14 A2**

392 King's Rd SW3. 071-351 2876. A purpose-built studio space on two levels. Enterprising management presents predominantly modern plays, often two different productions each

night. The pub is worth a visit in its own right. Performances *Tue-Sun.*

Old Red Lion
7 D1

418 St John St EC1. 071-837 7816. Upstairs studio theatre showing performances of new and exciting plays. Performances *Tue-Sun.*

Orange Tree

1 Clarence St, Richmond, Surrey. 081-940 3633. Highly successful fringe theatre which started life above the Victorian pub of the same name which is around the corner. Full range of productions – classics, revivals, new work and musicals. Performances *Mon-Sat.*

Pentameters
1 F1

Three Horseshoes, Heath St NW3. 071-431 7206. Box office: 071-435 3648. Classics, new works and occasional poetry readings. Performances *Tue-Sun.*

White Bear
15 E1

138 Kennington Park Rd SE11. 071-793 9193. Interesting programme that includes rediscovered writers and little-known works. Performances *Tue-Sun.*

LIVE MUSIC

The venues below vary enormously, from pubs where a pianist plays old-time favourites, to those where new or established bands perform in front of large audiences. The ones listed in this section are all well-established – but live entertainment is always subject to change, so do telephone in advance, or check the weekly music press or *Time Out* for full details.

In some cases, entertainment is free, but most pubs with a separate music room charge an entrance fee, which is normally around £5.00-£8.00, depending on the venue and who is playing.

Archway Tavern

Archway Close, Archway Roundabout N19. 071-272 2840. *Courage.* Comfortable pub with live music *nightly* and *Sun lunchtimes.* Traditional Irish bands. *Open to 24.00, to 23.30 Sun.* **B**

Biddy Mulligan's
1 D5

205 Kilburn High Rd NW6 071-624 2066. *Courage.* A mainly

Irish clientele gather in this charming, cosy pub. Irish cooking and live music – anything from traditional Irish to blues or rock 'n' roll – *every night. Open to 24.00.* **B**

Brahms & Liszt   11 B1
19 Russell St WC2. 071-240 3661. Live music beneath the wine bar *every night until 01.00.* Mainly blues and rock. Food available upstairs.

Brewery Tap
47 Catherine Wheel Rd, Brentford. 081-560 5200. *Fuller's.* Dinky pub by a tributary of the Thames. Jazz on *Tue & Thur evenings.* **B L D**

Bull & Gate   2 E3
389 Kentish Town Rd NW5. 071-485 5358. *Charrington.* Live music – mainly indie and rock – *every night* at the back of the pub. Real ales. **B** *(not Sat & Sun)*

Bull's Head
373 Lonsdale Rd SW13. 081-876 5241. *Youngs.* Large Victorian building overlooking the Thames where top international jazz musicians play *nightly* and *Sun lunchtimes.* Top quality jazz and excellent home cooking. **B L D** *(Reserve)*

Dover Street Wine Bar   6 E6
8-9 Dover St W1. 071-629 9813. Live music *Mon-Sat.* Jazz from *Mon-Wed;* R&B from *Thur-Sat.* A la carte restaurant. *Open to 03.00. Closed Sun.*

Dublin Castle   2 E5
94 Parkway NW1. 071-485 1773. *Courage.* Live music *nightly. Mon* is blues night, *Tue & Thur* are club nights for new bands, mainly indie and rock. The rest of the week can be anything from punk to R&B. Two bars. Dancefloor. *Open to 24.00.* **B**

🍺 Fox & Firkin
316 Lewisham High St SE13. 081-690 8925. *Firkin Brewery.* One of the Firkin chain of pubs, offering live music *Wed-Sat.* Guitar music on *Wed & Thur eves,* piano player on *Fri & Sat eves.* **B**

Half Moon   13 A6
93 Lower Richmond Rd SW15. 081-799 2387. *Youngs.* Large pub with spacious back room where live music is played *nightly* and on *Sun lunchtime.* Wide range of music including jazz, R&B, rock, folk and soul. Top names are billed here. **B**

Half Moon Hotel 18 F4
10 Half Moon Lane SE24. 071-274 2733. *Courage*. Ritzy, chintzy pub with a big public-cum-saloon bar and a licensed music room at the back which can hold up to 400. Local and visiting bands play a lively variety of rock, new wave, soul and R&B. Two sessions on *Sun*. Licence extends to *24.00 Thur-Sat*. **B** *(not eve)*

King's Head 13 B5
4 Fulham High St SW6. 071-736 1413. *Free House*. Large turn-of-the-century building with a fairytale turret in the middle. Live music, mainly rock and blues. *Open to 24.00 Thur-Sat*.

King's Head, Fulham

King's Head 3 E5
115 Upper St N1. 071-226 0364. *Taylor Walker*. Famous theatre pub which also has live music *nightly* after the stage performance. Folk, rock or jazz. **D** *(not Sun & Mon)*

London Globe 13 A2
175 Fulham Palace Rd W6. 071-381 8267. *Watneys*. Famous old pub with interior purpose-built for staging music. Rock and pop and a variety of other entertainment from *Mon-Sat*. **B**

Minogues   **3 D5**
80 Liverpool Rd N1. 071-359 4554. *Courage.* Beautifully decorated in belle epoch-style, this spacious pub is extremely popular. Irish meals are served in the lower seating area. Live music
every night, generally Irish, but also blues bands *Tue & Sun.*

Power Haus   **3 D6**
1 Liverpool Rd N1. 071-837 3218. *Charrington.* Once Sir Walter
Raleigh's house and reputedly one of the first buildings in
England to encounter tobacco smoke. Now a pleasant pub with
a lounge bar complete with stage and dancefloor. R&B or indie
every night. Traditional Irish music (free admission) *Sat & Sun
lunchtime.* Licensed *to 02.00.* **B**

Red Lion
318-322 High St, Brentford. 081-560 6181. *Fuller's.* Bands play
every night – usually R&B. Entry fee for the *evenings* but there
are also *Sun lunchtime* sessions which are free. *Open to 24.00
Mon-Thur, to 01.00 Fri & Sat.*

Ruskin Arms
386 High St North E12. 081-472 0377. *Charrington.* Large pub
with a boxing gymnasium upstairs and one or two well-known
boxing faces in the bar. Music hall where visiting bands play
heavy rock from *Thur-Sun.*

Sir George Robey
240 Seven Sisters Rd N4. 071-263 4581. *Taylor Walker.* Once
associated with the old Finsbury Park Empire where Marie
Lloyd, Harry Champion and George Robey played to packed
audiences. Robey himself is said to have drunk here. There's a
painting of him outside and the saloon is lined with photos of
his act. Irish-run now, with music *every night.* **B**

The Swan   **13 D3**
1 Fulham Bdwy SW6. 071-385 1840. *Courage.* A great venue
for R&B and rock bands *every night.* Some fairly well-known
bands have started out here. *Open to 24.00 Mon-Wed, to
02.00 Thur-Sat.* **B**

The Tankard   **11 D4**
111 Kennington Rd SE11. 071-735 1517. *Charrington.*
Opposite the Imperial War Museum. Comfortable and friendly
with pianist on *Fri, Sat & Sun,* often inspiring a sing-song. **B**

The Torrington Arms
4 Lodge Lane N12. 081-445 4710. *Whitbread.* Well-known on
the pub circuit for some top names in rock and blues. Resident

and visiting bands play on *Fri & Sun eves. Open to 24.00 Fri & Sun.* **B**

Tufnell Park Tavern   **2 G1**
162 Tufnell Park Rd N7. 071-272 2078. *Scottish & Newcastle.* The 1930s decor provides a suitable backdrop for the frequent jazz sessions on *Fri-Mon eves.* A popular pub serving real ale and good food. **B**

White Lion   **7 F3**
37 Central St EC1. 071-253 4975. *Whitbread.* Typical traditional East End pub with an impressive old grand piano on which classic sing-along songs are belted out from *Fri-Mon.* **B**

COMEDY

London's live cabaret circuit provides some of the capital's cheapest, liveliest grass-roots entertainment and many comedy clubs are to be found in the back rooms of pubs. Venues offering regular club nights are listed below, but the circuit is ever-changing, so do telephone in advance, or check *Time Out* for full details.

Acton Banana
King's Head, 214 High St W3. 081-673 8904. The Acton venue of the well-known Banana Cabaret (see below). Top comedians. Performances *Fri.*

Banana Cabaret   **17 E6**
Bedford, Bedford Hill SW12. 081-673 8904. Great venue, rated highly on the cabaret circuit. Top comedians. Performances *Fri & Sat.*

Cartoon at Clapham   **17 G2**
The Plough Inn, 196-198 Clapham High St SW4. 071-738 8763. Strong line-ups at this large, comfortable pub venue. Performances *Fri & Sat.*

Chuckle Club   **7 B3**
Marquis Cornwallis, 31 Marchmont St WC1. 071-476 1672. Top cabaret acts presented by compere Eugene Cheese. Also at The Shakespeare's Head, Carnaby St W1(**6 F6**). Performances *Sat.*

Comedy in Tatters   **11 B2**
PS Tattershall Castle, Victoria Embankment WC2. 071-733 6322. London's only floating comedy club. Performances *Sun.*

Downstairs at The King's Head

2 Crouch End Hill N8. 081-340 1028. A fine selection of acts in this club which has been a popular venue for live stand-up comedy for many years. Monthly try-out nights. Performances *Sat & Sun.*

Ealing Comedy Club

Drayton Court , 2 The Avenue, off Drayton Green Rd W13. 081-747 9129. Stand-up comedy and try-out spots. Performances *Sun.*

Comedy at The Drayton Court

East Dulwich Cabaret

East Dulwich Tavern, 1 Lordship Lane SE22. 081-299 4138. Quality comedy line-ups. Performances *Fri & Sat.*

Gate Theatre   9 D1

Prince Albert, 11 Pembridge Rd W11. 071-229 0706. Late-night improvised comedy shows. Performances *Sat.*

Guilty Pea   6 G5

The Wheatsheaf, 25 Rathbone Pl W1. 081-986 6861. Long-established venue offering new and established comedians. Performances *Sat.*

Meccano Club   3 E5

The Market Tavern, 2 Essex Rd N1. 081-800 2236. Good comedy, often from big names, in this pub basement. Improvisation a speciality. Performances *Fri & Sat.*

New Black Cat Cabaret
The Samuel Beckett, Stoke Newington Church St N16. 081-806 8779. Good value variety night at popular watering hole. Performances *Sun*.

Oranje Boom Boom   **6 G6**
De Hems, 11 Macclesfield St, off Shaftesbury Ave W1. 081-694 1710. Stand-up comedy and variety from established and new acts. Performances *Wed*.

Pub Next Door   **4 E3**
The Samuel Pepys, 289 Mare St E8. 081-985 2424. New variety comedy and 'open spots' for newcomers in this pub next door to the Hackney Empire. Performances *Fri*.

Screaming Blue Murder   **16 B2**
Slug & Lettuce, 14 Putney High St SW15. 081-339 0506. Comedy, music and stand-ups, chaired by a resident MC. Performances *Thur*. Also clubs at The Leather Bottle, 277 Kingston Rd, Wimbledon SW19 *(Sun)*, and at The Ferry Boat Tavern, 6 Bridge Rd, Hampton, Surrey *(Fri)*.

What the Dickens   **12 D2**
Dickens Inn, St Katharine's Way E1. 071-488 1226. Weekly comedy club with line-ups featuring new and experienced comics. Performances *Thur*.

Wimbledon Fortnight Club
The Castle, 27 Church Rd SW19. 081-747 9129. Fortnightly club with at least three comedy acts every show. Performances *Wed*.

GAY PUBS

London's gay and lesbian scene is one of Europe's biggest and best. The capital boasts an eclectic mix of pubs, clubs and bars and the best way to find out what's going on is to pick up a copy of one of the free newspapers such as *Capital Gay* or *The Pink Paper*. A reliable source of information on all gay venues is *Gay Switchboard* on 071-837 7324.

The Angel   **3 E6**
65 Graham St N1. *Free House*. Plush, comfortable decor at this revamped pub which used to be The Fallen Angel. Popular with a mixed, local crowd. *Open to 24.00 Mon-Sat, to 23.30 Sun*.

The Bell   **7 C1**
259 Pentonville Rd N1. 071-837 5617. *Charrington*. Spacious pub with an easy-going crowd and an alternative disco

nightly. Women-only on *Tue.* Open to 02.30 Thur-Sat, to 01.00 Sun.

📍 The Black Cap   2 F5
171 Camden High St NW1. 071-485 1742. *Charrington.* Popular drag pub with dancefloor and entertainment *six nights a week.* Quieter bar upstairs. *Open to 02.00, to 22.30 Sun.*

📍 The Champion   5 E6
1 Bayswater Rd W2. 071-229 5056. *Charrington.* Large bar and snuggery. Frequented by a lively crowd. Taped music. Popular with male gay locals. Occasional live entertainment including stripper nights.

📍 Comptons   6 G5
53 Old Compton St W1. 071-437 4445. *Charrington.* Large Soho pub with a comfortable and friendly atmosphere. *Closed Sun.*

Crews   7 B6
14 Upper St Martin's Lane WC2. 071-379 4880. *Charrington.* Huge, busy pub with a dark, club-like atmosphere.

Drill Hall   7 A4
16 Chenies St WC1. 071-631 1353. Busy bar in an arts centre with theatre and restaurant. Women-only *Mon.* **L D**

The Edge   6 G5
11 Soho Sq W1. 071-439 1223. Mixed gay/straight bar on two levels. *Open to 01.00, to 22.30 Sun.* **B**

📍 Gloucester
King William Walk SE10. 081-858 2666. *Charrington.* Next to one of the entrances to Greenwich Park, this pub is a gay venue *in the evenings* with cabaret acts *at weekends.*

📍 Goldsmith's Tavern
36 New Cross Rd SE14. 081-692 3648. *Courage.* A lively pub with a reputation for its disco, drag acts and alternative cabaret nights. *Wed, Fri & Sat* are the nights for gay-oriented cabaret. **B**

King's Arms   6 F5
23 Poland St W1. 071-734 5907. *Scottish & Newcastle.* Busy, friendly gay men's pub. The upstairs bar is quieter.

📍 King William IV   1 G1
77 Hampstead High St NW3. 071-435 5747. *Courage.* Traditional Hampstead pub with one large oak-panelled bar and a beer garden out at the back. Predominantly gay men.

Kudos 7 B6

10 Adelaide St, off William IV St WC2. 071-379 4573. Gay café/bar which is always packed in the evening. Tea, coffee and food served during the day. **B**

Market Tavern 15 B2

Market Towers, 1 Nine Elms Lane SW8. 071-622 5655. *Free House.* Thought of by many as the best gay pub in south London. Men-only nights *Mon & Wed. Open to 02.00 Mon-Thur, to 03.00 Fri & Sat, to 24.00 Sun.*

Queen's Head 10 C6

27 Tryon St SW3. 071-589 0262. *Scottish & Newcastle.* Traditional pub with three bars, two of which attract a mixed gay crowd. **B** *(not eve)*

Recessions 7 B3

Brunswick Centre, Russell Sq WC1. 071-833 8554. *Courage.* Friendly gay-owned pub open to a mixed crowd. Women-only *Sat.*

Royal Oak

62 Glenthorne Rd W6. 081-748 2781. *Free House.* Large art deco pub with entertainment *Mon-Thur & Sun nights* and *Sun lunchtime. Mon* is karaoke night, *Wed night* is "girls on top", but expect a mixed crowd. Strippers perform the rest of the week. *Open to 01.00 Mon, to 24.00 Tue & Wed, to 02.00 Thur & Fri* and *all day to 24.00 Sun.* **B**

Royal Vauxhall Tavern 11 C6

372 Kennington Lane SE11. 071-582 0833. *Courage.* Noisy, friendly pub which was the first in London to produce regular drag shows. Mostly male gays. *Open from 20.00-24.00 Mon-Thur, to 02.00 Fri & Sat.* **B**

Two Brewers 17 G2

114 Clapham High St SW4. 071-622 3621. *Charrington.* Big on entertainment with cabaret and drag shows *Mon, Wed, Thur & Fri eve,* and also at *Sun lunchtime.* Mainly evening trade, very quiet at lunchtime. *Open to 01.00 Mon-Thur, to 02.00 Fri & Sat, to 24.00 Sun.*

Village Soho 5 G5

81 Wardour St W1. 071-434 2123. Newer, bigger sister of Village West One (see below), with three bars on two levels. Winner of *The Pink Paper* Best Bar of the Year Award. Attracts a young crowd. **B** *(not eve)*

Village West One 6 G5

38 Hanway St W1. 071-436 2468. Slickly decorated with a Mediterranean feel. Murals of well-toned and semi-clothed men adorn the walls. **B** *(not eve)*

LATE-NIGHT DRINKING

There aren't many places in London where you can drink after pub closing time. The exceptions are restaurants, where you normally have to eat a full meal, and nightclubs, which generally charge an admission fee. The following is a list of bars with last orders *after 24.00.*

See also *Brasseries & cafés* section – some are *open to 24.00* – and *Live music* section – many pubs obtain licence extensions when bands are playing.

Bar Madrid   **6 F5**
4 Winsley St, off Oxford St W1. 071-436 4649. Large and lively tapas bar with a wine bar above which serves alcohol until *03.00. Closed Sun.*

Bar Sol Ona   **6 G5**
17 Old Compton St W1. 071-287 9932. Basement bar attracting a party crowd. Tapas, flamenco music. *Open to 02.00. Closed Sun.*

Blushes Café   **14 C1**
52 King's Rd SW3. 071-589 6640. A French-style café/brasserie with live music *at weekends. Open to 24.00, to 04.00 Thur-Sat.*

Café Bohème   **6 G5**
13 Old Compton St W1. 071-734 0623. Right in the heart of Soho, you can order your last drink at *02.00* at this lively brasserie/bar. *Open to 03.00.*

Café Pelican   **7 B6**
45 St Martin's Lane WC2. 071-379 0309. Relaxed atmosphere with piano jazz in the background. *Open to 02.00.*

Cuba Libre   **3 E5**
72 Upper St N1. 071-354 9998. Bar/restaurant with live Latin music most evenings. *Open to 02.00 Tue-Sat, to 24.00 Sun & Mon.*

Dover Street Wine Bar   **6 E6**
8-9 Dover St W1. 071-491 7509. Basement wine bar with live jazz or R&B *every night. Open to 03.00. Closed Sun.*

EARLY-OPENING PUBS

Even with the relaxed licensing laws there are not many pubs which choose to open for business at *06.00* in the morning. The exceptions are, and always have been, those which are close to the major wholesale markets. Smithfield wholesale meat market is well served, as are New Covent Garden market, Borough Market and Stratford Market. Special licences allow alcohol to be served to bona fide market workers.

Some pubs in central London open early to serve traditional English breakfast.

Barley Mow   **15 B2**
East Bridge, New Covent Garden Market SW8. 071-720 5555. *Courage.* Serves full breakfasts, full lunches and snacks. The customers are predominantly shift workers and traders from New Covent Garden fruit, vegetable and flower market, which moved here in 1974. *Open 05.00-15.00. Closed Sat & Sun.* **B**

Fox & Anchor   **7 E4**
115 Charterhouse St EC1. 071-253 4838. *Taylor Walker.* Behind a moulded stone art nouveau façade is a friendly old bar with separate restaurant section serving huge breakfasts and grilled lunches to the buyers and butchers of nearby Smithfield. It's a jolly place, always resounding with the chatter and laughter of market workers. It is advisable to book for the set breakfast. *Open 06.00-22.00. Closed Sat & Sun.* **B L**

The Globe   **11 G2**
8 Bedale St SE1. 071-407 0043. *Free House.* Handy for the fruit and vegetable dealers of Borough Market who can enjoy coffee, liqueurs, Draught Bass or a guest real ale in the early hours. *Open 11.00-21.00 Mon; 06.30-08.30 & 11.00-21.00 Tue-Sat. Closed Sun.*

The Hope Tavern   **7 E4**
94 Cowcross St EC1. 071-250 1442. *Courage.* Pretty 19th-century pub near Smithfield Market. Serves great breakfasts and traditional English lunches in the upstairs restaurant. *Open 06.00-18.00. Closed Sat & Sun.* **B L**

Newmarket   **7 E4**
26 Smithfield St, off Snow Hill EC1. 071-248 2464. *Charrington.* Always bustling and crowded with workers from nearby Smithfield Market. *Open 06.30-09.30 & 11.00-23.00. Closed Sat & Sun.* **B**

🍺 Railway Tavern
131 Angel Lane E15. 071-534 3123. *Charrington.* Amiable old Victorian pub with a comfortable bar and a games room for pool and darts. The early session is for the benefit of the Stratford wholesale fruit and vegetable market. Beer garden, patio and real ale. *Open 06.00-08.00 & 11.00-23.00 Mon-Sat; 12.00-15.00 & 19.00-22.30 Sun.* **B**

The following pubs open early for traditional English breakfast:

🍺 Albert   10 F4
52 Victoria St SW1. 071-222 5577. *Scottish & Newcastle.* Serves breakfast *08.00-10.30 Mon-Fri.*

🍺 Chandos   7 B6
29 St Martin's Lane WC2. 071-836 1401. *Samuel Smith.* Next to the English National Opera on St Martin's Lane, this huge Victorian pub serves breakfast from *09.00 Mon-Sun. Open all day Sun.*

Fox & Anchor   7 E4
115 Charterhouse St EC1. 071-253 4838. *Taylor Walker.* Serves breakfast *07.00-10.30 Mon-Fri.*

Gloucester   10 C4
187 Sloane St SW1. 071-235 0298. *Scottish & Newcastle.* Serves traditional or continental breakfast *08.00-11.30 Mon-Sat.*

BARS

Bars are generally noisier and busier than pubs, and are particularly popular with party crowds. Imported beers and cocktails can be expensive, but most bars run happy hours, normally around *18.00* as the after-work drinking crowds arrive, when drinks are cheaper, often half-price. Many bars also have extended licensing hours.

B in this section means that some kind of food is served, but this can vary enormously from snacks to full meals, so it is always advisable to check in advance.

Bar Sol   11 B1
11-12 Russell St WC2. 071-240 5330. This basement bar is always busy. Spanish wines, Mexican beers, crushed ice margueritas and other cocktails. Selection of tapas and bar snacks. Latin music. **B**

Beach Blanket Babylon   5 D5
45 Ledbury Rd W11. 071-229 2907. Very stylish bar attracting a particularly trendy crowd. Through imposing iron doors is a huge room dominated by a walk-around bar. Interesting design features are roaring lion's mouth fireplaces, Grecian pots filled with dried flowers, gilt-edged mirrors, statues. Bottled beers and wine.

Boardwalk   6 G5
18 Greek St W1. 071-287 2051. Lively bar/restaurant, in the heart of Soho, which is always crowded. Loud music and a disco downstairs. Food is an unusual mix of American and French cuisine. **B**

Café Pacifico   7 B5
5 Langley St, off Long Acre WC2. 071-379 7728. Bar/restaurant built in a converted warehouse. Has a long and welcoming bar serving margueritas, over a dozen tequilas, and Mexican beers. Latin music. **B**

Circa   6 E6
Lansdowne House, 59 Berkeley Sq W1. 071-499 7850. Glossy, stylish bar, on the ground floor of the Saatchi & Saatchi building, therefore popular with advertising people. Extensive wine list, excellent bar snacks. **B**

📍 **Cuba Libre**   **3 E5**
72 Upper St N1. 071-354 9998. Buzzing atmosphere at this popular bar and restaurant. Brazilian, Chilean, Mexican, Spanish and Portuguese wines, plus beers and cocktails. Live Cuban music. **B**

📍 **The Dog House**   **6 G5**
187 Wardour St W1. 071-434 2116. Lively basement bar in Soho decorated in every colour imaginable. Their speciality is flavoured vodkas. Also cocktails and bottled beers. **B**

📍 **The Fifth Floor**   **10 C3**
Harvey Nichols, Knightsbridge SW1. 071-235 5250. This welcoming bar is a cross between a hotel lounge bar and a slick cocktail bar. The large horseshoe bar is stocked with 20 vodkas and 52 whiskies, and there is a large range of cocktails on offer.

📍 **Freuds**   **7 B5**
198 Shaftesbury Ave WC2. 071-240 9933. You climb down an iron staircase to get to this relaxed basement bar. Cocktails, imported beers, bar snacks and finger nibbles. **B**

📍 **Henry J Bean's (But His Friends All
Call Him Hank) Bar & Grill**
195-197 King's Rd SW3. 071-352 9255.   **14 B1**
490 Fulham Rd SW6. 071-381 5005.   **13 D3**
54 Abingdon Rd W8. 071-937 3339.   **9 D4**
One of the original American-style cocktail bars. Big and noisy, with high stools and 1950s American memorabilia on the walls. A huge list of house cocktails and a variety of American beers. **B**

📍 **Maxwell's**
9 James St, off Floral St WC2. 071-836 0303.   **7 B6**
76 Heath St NW3. 071-794 5450.   **1 F1**
The lively atmosphere and loud rock music attract a young crowd. Good selection of cocktails, and American-sized drinks measures. **B**

📍 **Old Orleans**
29-31 Wellington St WC2. 071-497 2433.   **11 C1**
64 Heath St NW3. 071-794 0122.   **1 F1**
26-42 Bond St W5. 081-579 7413.
8 Queen's Rd, Richmond, Surrey. 081-940 1306.
Huge, lively and bustling, designed to re-create the feel of New Orleans. American and Mexican beers, plus expertly-mixed cocktails. **B**

📍 **Rumours**   **11 C1**
33 Wellington St WC2. 071-836 0038. The main bar here is in a large, pillared room surrounded by mirrors. Two basement

bars. All serving an imaginative range of modern and classic cocktails.Extensive happy hours.

TGI Friday's
6 Bedford St WC2. 071-379 0585.   **7 B6**
29 Coventry St W1. 071-839 6262.   **10 G1**
Loud and lively bar/restaurant with American themed decor. A huge range of cocktails, alcoholic and non-alcoholic. **B**

HOTEL BARS

The American Bar   **7 C6**
Savoy Hotel, Strand WC2. 071-836 4343. Sophisticated and stylish with waiters in white stewards' jackets serving an enormous range of expertly mixed cocktails. A pianist and singer entertain *Mon-Sat evenings.*

Athenaeum Bar   **10 E2**
Athenaeum Hotel, Piccadilly W1. 071-499 3464. Mellow wood-panelled bar which has London's largest selection of single malt whiskies. The cocktail list includes all the classics but the bar staff will mix whatever you ask for.

Café Royal   **10 F1**
68 Regent St W1. 071-437 9090. Refined elegance in the cocktail bar, which is popular with smart businessmen and tourists. Champagne-based cocktails are the speciality.

Churchill's Bar   **6 D5**
Churchill Hotel, Portman Sq W1. 071-486 5800. Beautiful bar in a Regency-style room. The specially-commissioned murals of Oriental sporting scenes blend subtly with the deep red fittings. Devilish Bloody Marys, very dry Martinis and an impressive Churchill No.10 Special.

Palm Court   **10 F2**
The Ritz, Piccadilly W1. 071-493 8181. Designed by Cesar Ritz himself, this splendid baroque room with its central gold leaf fountain is straight from a bygone era. Ever popular is the vodka or gin Ricci – synonymous with the Ritz in the cocktail heyday.

Trader Vic's   **10 D2**
Hilton Hotel, 22 Park Lane W1. 071-493 8000. There are branches of Trader Vic's all over the world. The London branch has a sultry South Sea island setting complete with bamboo, fishing nets and Hawaiian-shirted waiters. An enormous range of exotic brews, many of them rum-based, served in extravagant bowls and adorned with floating flowers.

BRASSERIES & CAFES

Continental-style brasseries and cafés are a welcome addition to pubs and bars in London. They offer informal, stylish surroundings where you will find good food and alcoholic drinks (which you can consume without having to eat). Most have taken advantage of the relaxed licensing laws which allow them to stay open all day.

All entries in this section serve some kind of food, but this can vary enormously from snacks to full meals, so it is always advisable to check in advance.

🍵 La Brasserie   10 B5
272 Brompton Rd SW3. 071-584 1668. Probably one of the closest things to a real French brasserie in London. Open for breakfast and throughout the day for coffee and pâtisseries – newspapers provided.

🍵 The Brasserie   17 B6
11 Bellevue Rd SW17. 081-767 6982. Large bay windows at the front overlooking Wandsworth Common and seating on the pavement in summer. Restaurant serves mainly French dishes.

🍵 Brasserie du Coin   7 C3
54 Lamb's Conduit St WC1. 071-405 1717. Typical French brasserie with wooden floors and candlelit tables. You can get light snacks such as filled baguettes or classic French dishes.

🍵 Brasserie Lott   10 C4
27-31 Basil St SW3. 071-584 4484. Just behind Harrods, this attractive brasserie has a modern menu and a café next door which serves breakfasts, light snacks and more substantial dishes. *Closed Sun.*

🍵 Brasserie du Marché aux Puces   5 B4
349 Portobello Rd W10. 081-968 5828. Trendy and minimalist, this brasserie is pleasantly light and airy due to its street-corner position. Very busy on a Saturday with custom from the nearby Portobello Market. Full meals, snacks and pastries available all day. Sunday brunch.

Brasserie Rocque
8 B4

37 Broadgate Circle EC2. 071-638 7919. Smart, modern brasserie overlooking the Broadgate development. Very busy at lunchtimes with City office workers. Modern French food. *Closed Sat & Sun.*

Brompton Brasserie
13 F2

224 Fulham Rd SW10. 071-351 3956. Relaxed, friendly atmosphere and a varied menu. They also serve afternoon teas and Sunday brunch. Lengthy wine list.

Café des Amis du Vin
7 B5

11-14 Hanover Pl, off Long Acre WC2. 071-379 3444. This extremely popular brasserie is sandwiched between a wine bar in the basement and the elegant Salon des Amis du Vin restaurant upstairs. Good range of French, German, Spanish and Californian wines.

Le Café des Amis du Vin

Café Bohème
6 G5

13 Old Compton St W1. 071-734 0623. Pleasantly chaotic French-style brasserie in the heart of Soho which attracts a young crowd. You can have a cappuccino, a beer, snacks such as croque monsieur and omelettes, or a full meal.

Café Casbar   7 B5
52 Earlham St WC2. 071-379 7768. Modern, attractive café enlivened by an evening club which runs monthly exhibitions of art for viewing and sale, games nights and poetry readings. Breakfasts, salads, sandwiches, hot daily specials.

Café Delancey   2 E5
3 Delancey St NW1. 071-387 1985. Relaxed, European-style brasserie with a sophisticated, bohemian appeal. You can have any dish you like, whatever the time of day. Breakfasts, brunches, delicious cakes and coffee, unusual daily specials.

Café Flo
- 51 St Martin's Lane WC2. 071-836 8289.   7 B6
- 127 Kensington Church St W8. 071-727 8142.   9 D2
- 676 Fulham Rd SW6. 071-371 9673.   13 C4
- 205 Haverstock Hill NW3. 071-435 6744.   2 C3
- 334 Upper St N1. 071-226 7916.   3 E5
- 149 Kew Rd, Richmond, Surrey. 081-940 8298.
A growing chain of chic Parisian-style cafés. Continental and English breakfasts, bistro snacks, simple set meals, French classics. Well-selected wine list.

Café Italien (des Amis du Vin)   6 F4
19 Charlotte St W1. 071-636 4174. Charming brasserie with a good choice of Italian, French and Californian wines. Also a restaurant and wine bar.

Café Météor   13 A2
158 Fulham Palace Rd W6. 081-741 5037. Authentic, informal brasserie with a wide range of snacks and more substantial dishes.

Café Pelican   7 B6
45 St Martin's Lane WC2. 071-379 0309. Lively and noisy theatreland brasserie with tables spilling onto the pavement outside. Inside is divided into two sections; you can have snacks and drinks at the front, and full meals at the back. Jazz pianist nightly from *21.00.*

Café Rouge   5 C6
31 Kensington Park Rd W11. 071-221 4449. One of a chain of Parisian-style cafés with a warm and welcoming atmosphere. Breakfast, croissants and baguettes, salads and sandwiches or full brasserie meals. French wine list. Numerous branches.

Café Royal Brasserie   10 F1
68 Regent St W1. 071-437 9090. The brasserie in this most famous of cafés serves classic French brasserie fare in elegant

surroundings. All manner of alcoholic and non-alcoholic drinks.

Café St Pierre
7 D3

29 Clerkenwell Green EC1. 071-251 6606. This ground floor brasserie is welcoming and bright. Well chosen wines. French cuisine in the upstairs restaurant.

Camden Brasserie
2 E5

216 Camden High St NW1. 071-482 2114. A relaxed atmosphere at this popular brasserie near the canal. Quality Mediterranean food. An open fire in winter adds to the relaxed ambience.

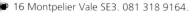 **Covent Garden Brasserie**
7 B6

1 The Piazza, Covent Garden WC2. 071-240 6654. Parisian-style café with glassed-in seating in winter, opening onto the pavement in summer. Snacks and more substantial French and Italian dishes. Also open for breakfast *(summer only)* and afternoon tea. Good wine list, mostly French.

Dôme

38 Long Acre WC2. 071-836 0701. **7 B6**
34 Wellington St WC2. 071-836 7823. **11 C1**
290-291 Regent St W1. 071-636 7006. **6 E5**
354 King's Rd SW3. 071-352 7611. **13 G2**
341 Upper St, N1. 071-226 3414. **3 E5**
38-39 Hampstead High St NW3. 071-435 4240. **1 F1**
98-100 Shepherd's Bush Rd W6. 071-602 7732.
85 Strand on the Green W4. 081-995 6575.
16 Montpelier Vale SE3. 081 318 9164.

Dôme

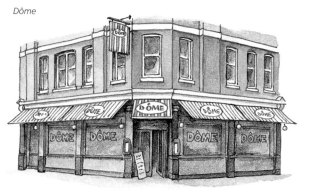

This successful chain of brasseries named after the famous Paris Dôme has branches all over London, distinguished by their brown and cream striped canopies. Standard brasserie fare in a friendly, lively atmosphere.

🍴 Flumbs   **17 F4**
67-69 Abbeville Rd SW4. 081-675 2201. Brasserie/café/wine bar serving breakfasts, brunches, pastries, bar snacks, afternoon teas and full meals from a modern British menu.

🍴 Soho Brasserie   **6 G5**
23-25 Old Compton St W1. 071-439 9301. Pub conversion with an arty French interior and trendy clientele. Coffee, drinks and snacks at the front bar, which in summer opens on to the pavement. Full meals are served in the large modern brasserie-style dining room at the back.

🍴 Soho Soho   **6 G5**
11-13 Frith St W1. 071-494 3491. A glass-fronted wine bar/brasserie with a French restaurant upstairs and a rotisserie downstairs. Always lively. Outside tables.

🍴 Tuttons   **11 B1**
11-12 Russell St WC2. 071-836 4141. Right on the edge of the Covent Garden Piazza, this is a large, airy brasserie with a good, reasonably priced English/international menu and a relaxed atmosphere. Plenty of tables outside on the piazza. Atmospheric cellar bar.

🍴 WKD Café   **2 E4**
18 Kentish Town Rd NW1. 071-267 1869. This popular north London café serves simple, well-prepared food during the day. You can read the papers or play chess while you drink cappuccinos and eat open sandwiches. The fuller menu has salads and hot daily specials. There is also a breakfast club; enjoy English or continental breakfast to the accompaniment of live jazz. In the evening the café becomes a club.

WINE BARS

Wine bars are a well-established alternative to the good old English pub. From the vast selection in London the following includes those establishments with good wines and a relaxed atmosphere. Most carry a range of well-known wines, a few unusual bottles and at least one reliable house wine. Almost all offer wine by the glass but it usually works out cheaper to buy a bottle. They all serve food – cheese, pâté, quiche and salads are typical wine bar fare – although some serve more substantial food or have restaurants of their own. It is advisable to check in advance what is available.

Wine bars are now able to stay open all day (except *Sun)* if they choose, though some still close for a few hours in the afternoon. Many of those in the City *close early at around 21.00 and are closed on Sat & Sun.*

Actor's Retreat   **7 E2**
326 St John St EC1. 071-837 0722. Popular family-owned wine bar. Attractive interior; ceramic-tiled walls, old beams, an original fireplace and numerous photos of actors and actresses. Good range of Spanish and Italian wines. *Closed Sun.*

Andrew Edmunds   **6 F6**
46 Lexington St W1. 071-437 5708. Small but charming wine bar/restaurant which serves excellent wines and imaginative food.

Archduke   **11 C2**
Concert Hall Approach SE1. 071-928 9370. Built into two railway arches underneath Waterloo Bridge, this wine bar serves excellent food; the restaurant upstairs specialises in sausages from all over the world. Live jazz *nightly. Closed lunchtime Sat & all day Sun.*

L'Artiste Musclé   **10 E2**
1 Shepherd Market, off White Horse St W1. 071-493 6150. A cheap and cheerful French wine bar/bistro, particularly appealing in summer when you can sit outside at the pavement tables. Well-prepared French menu and a fine selection of cheeses. *Closed lunchtime Sun.*

Balls Brothers

One of the oldest wine bar chains in London with most of its branches in the City. They share a common list of more than 60 wines, with the occasional fine claret or Burgundy. Food and its availability varies from bar to bar. Most branches *close early at around 21.00 and are closed on Sat & Sun. Check with individual branches for times*. Balls Brothers have a wine centre offering good value wines from around the world at 313 Cambridge Heath Rd E2 (**8 F3**), 071-739 6466.

3 Budge Row, Cannon St EC2. 071-248 7557.	**7 G6**
5 Carey Lane, off Foster Lane EC2. 071-600 2720.	**7 F5**
6 Cheapside EC2. 071-248 2708.	**7 F5**
Gows Restaurant, 81 Old Broad St EC2. 071-920 9645.	**8 A5**
Great Eastern Hotel, Liverpool St EC2. 071-626 7919.	**8 B4**
Hay's Galleria, Tooley St SE1. 071-407 4301.	**12 B2**
The Hop Cellars, 24 Southwark St. 071-403 6851.	**11 F2**
King's Arms Yard, off Coleman St EC2. 071-796 3049.	**7 G5**
Moor House, London Wall EC2. 071-628 3944.	**7 F4**
2 Old Change Ct, St Paul's Churchyard EC4. 071-248 8697.	**7 F5**
20 St James's St SW1. 071-321 0882.	**10 F2**
St Mary at Hill EC3. 071-626 0321.	**12 B1**
42 Threadneedle St EC2. 071 628 3050.	**8 A5**

🍷 Bar des Amis   7 B5

11-14 Hanover Pl, off Long Acre WC2. 071-379 3444. An extremely popular wine bar below the Café des Amis du Vin brasserie and the elegant Salon des Amis du Vin restaurant. The wine list includes over 20 wines from the New World, plus monthly specials. *Closed Sun.*

🍷 Basil's   10 C3

Basil Street Hotel, 8 Basil St SW3. 071-581 3311. A vaulted cellar with arches which you enter by way of an imposing iron staircase. Bar along one side and café-style seating along the other. Interesting menu. *Closed Sat eve and all day Sun.*

🍷 Le Beaujolais   7 B6

25 Litchfield St WC2. 071-836 2955. Lively, mixed clientele in this popular and intimate French wine bar. The wine list includes their own-label house white and red plus, of course, Beaujolais. Authentic French cooking. *Closed Sun.*

Betjeman's
7 E4

44 Cloth Fair, Smithfield EC1. 071-796 4981. Housed in the Jacobean home of former Poet Laureate John Betjeman, this excellent wine bar boasts a range of bar snacks, a full restaurant menu and an extensive wine list. The Betjeman Society holds meetings here. *Closed Sat & Sun.*

Bill Bentley's Wine Bar
10 B4

31 Beauchamp Pl SW3. 071-589 5080. Below a superb fish restaurant, the wine bar here is cosy and old-fashioned with a relaxed atmosphere. There's an oyster bar serving delicious and well-presented snacks including fish cakes and potted shrimps. Patio garden. Branch at 18 Old Broad St EC2 (**8 B5**). 071-588 2655. *Closed Sun.*

Bleeding Heart
7 D4

Bleeding Heart Yard, off Greville St EC1. 071-242 8238. The Bleeding Heart features in Dickens' *Little Dorrit* so it's only natural that Dickens prints and first editions are to be found here. Excellent wine list. *Closed Sat & Sun.*

Booty's Riverside Bar

92a Narrow St E14. 071-987 8343. Once a pub called the Waterman's Arms, this was one of the first places in the redevelopment of the Docklands area to turn itself into a wine bar. Reasonable selection of 50 wines, good wholesome food. River views from the back. *Closed Sun eve.*

Bow Wine Vaults
7 F5

10 Bow Churchyard, off Cheapside EC4. 071-248 1121. Victorian bar within the sound of Bow Bells. Popular with City workers for its wide selection of wines; over a hundred French, Spanish, German and Californian wines. Also fortified wines and malt whiskies. Snacks and excellent cheeses. *Closed Sat & Sun.*

Brahms & Liszt
11 B1

19 Russell St WC2. 071-240 3661. Lively, crowded Covent Garden wine bar with live music downstairs. Wide selection of wines and a good range of hot food. Downstairs *open to 01.00, to 22.30 Sun.*

Carriages
10 E4

43 Buckingham Palace Rd SW1. 071-834 8871. This wine bar is opposite the Queen's carriage house. The lowered ceiling, low brick walls and wrought-ironwork create an interesting and unusual effect. Innovative bar menu. Restaurant downstairs. *Closed Sat & Sun.*

🍷 **Cork & Bottle**   **7 A6**
44-46 Cranbourn St WC2. 071-734 7807. Invariably crowded cellar bar just off Leicester Square. The walls are covered with posters of wines and champagnes. Excellent selection of wines and bar snacks. Also hot dishes. *Open to 24.00, to 22.30 Sun.*

🍷 **Crusting Pipe**   **7 B6**
27 The Market, Covent Garden WC2. 071-836 1415. Very popular wine bar, part of the Davy's chain (see below). Outside seating under the piazza canopy. Good food, including grills and bar snacks, and reasonably-priced wines. *Closed Sun eve.*

Daniel's   **10 F1**
68 Regent St W1. 071-437 9090. At the back of the Café Royal, this pleasant, relaxed wine bar has a resident pianist, a varied wine list and conventional bar snacks. *Closed Sat & Sun.*

Davy's
Dusty barrels, old prints and sawdust-covered floors create the Victorian image of these wine bars, the names of which date back to the wine trade of 100 years ago. The chain offers a good selection of wines and excellent food. Port, sherry and Madeira from the wood, sound French and German wines by the glass, fine wines by the bottle. The claret list is generally stronger than the Burgundy, but both are exceptional and moderately priced. Particularly noteworthy are the blackboard special offers. These may include Grand Cru clarets or Grande Marque champagne. The City bars *close at 20.00 or 20.30 and at weekends. Check with individual branches for times. All branches closed Sun.*
The following list is a selection:

Boot & Flogger   **11 F3**
10 Redcross Way SE1. 071-407 1184.
Bottlescrue   **7 E5**
Bath House, Holborn Viaduct EC1. 071-248 2157.
Bung Hole   **7 C4**
55-57 High Holborn WC1. 071-242 4318.
City Boot   **7 G4**
7 Moorfields High Walk, Moorgate EC2. 071-628 2360.
City Flogger   **8 B6**
120 Fenchurch St EC3. 071-623 3214.
Davy's   **7 E5**
10 Creed Lane, off Ludgate Hill EC4. 071-236 5861.
Davy's Wine Vaults
165 Greenwich High Rd SE10. 081-858 7204.
Gyngleboy   **5 G5**
27 Spring St W2. 071-723 3351.
Skinkers   **12 B2**
42 Tooley St SE1. 071-407 7720.

The Spittoon   **7 E4**
15-17 Long Lane EC1. 071-726 8858.

Tappit Hen   **7 B6**
5 William IV St WC2. 071-836 9811.

Udder Place   **7 F5**
Russia Court, Russia Row, 1-6 Milk St, off Gresham St EC2. 071-600 2165.

Dover Street Wine Bar   **6 E6**
8-9 Dover St W1. 071-629 9813. This large basement wine bar with its arched vaults is renowned for top-quality live music; jazz, blues and soul, played *six nights a week from 22.00.* There is a good wine list, snack menu and an à la carte restaurant open at lunchtime and for evening meals. *Open to 03.00. Closed Sun.*

Downs   **4 F3**
Arch 166, Bohemia Pl E8. 081-986 4325. Reasonably-priced east London wine bar housed in a converted railway arch. Candelit tables make for an intimate atmosphere.

● **Ebury Wine Bar**   **10 E5**
139 Ebury St SW1. 071-730 5447. Popular wine bar which is always crowded and lively. Comprehensive wine list and good selection of reasonably-priced food. Various wines of the week. Also beers and spirits.

Fenchurch Colony Wine Bar   **8 B6**
14 New London St, off Fenchurch St EC3. 071-481 0848. Comfortable, colonial-style decor in this slick wine bar with separate champagne bar. Popular with City office workers. Wine list is predominantly French but there are also choices from Italy, Germany, Australia and New Zealand. Specialises in enormous sandwiches. More elaborate dishes too. *Closed Sat & Sun.*

Five Lamps   **8 B6**
3 Railway Pl, off Fenchurch St EC3. 071-488 1587. Next door to Fenchurch Street Station, this basement wine bar offers a good selection of French, Italian and German wines. *Closed Sat & Sun.*

● **Gordon's Wine Bar**   **11 B2**
47 Villiers St WC2. 071-930 1408. This famous 300-year-old wine cellar has escaped demolition on more than one occasion, much to the relief of its regulars. The ancient stone walls and ceilings often drip with water but this just adds to the charm of the place. Excellent selection of wines, ports and sherries, plus wholesome buffet food. *Closed Sat & Sun.*

● Holborn Colony Wine Bar   7 D4
33 Brooke St EC1. 071-430 0677. Part of the same chain as the Fenchurch Colony Wine Bar (see above). In this one you'll find colonial-style decor and a well-balanced wine list. Hot and cold food and they also do the famous 'fat' Colony sandwiches. *Open to 20.00. Closed Sat & Sun.*

● Jimmie's Wine Bar   9 E3
18 Kensington Church St W8. 071-937 9988. Long, stable-like bar which is always busy. Sound house wines with a list notable for its fine claret. Live music in the evenings.

● Maxie's   10 C3
143 Knightsbridge SW1. 071-225 2553. Popular Knightsbridge wine bar with carefully selected wine list and an original line in Oriental snacks – Peking Duck and chicken saté make a welcome change from pâté and quiche. The separate restaurant area has a more extensive menu. Latin American night on *Thur;* Russian night on *Sat.*

192   5 C6
192 Kensington Park Rd W11. 071-229 0482. Wine bar at street level has an international wine list which includes several champagnes. Underground is the excellent restaurant offering an eclectic menu. *Open to 23.30.*

Pitcher & Piano
● 18-20 Chiswick High Rd W4. 081-742 7731.
● 214-216 Fulham Rd SW10. 071-352 9234.   **13 F2**
● 871-873 Fulham Rd SW6. 071-736 3910.   **13 B5**
● 8 Balham Hill SW12. 081-673 1107.   **17 E4**
Pleasant and airy wine bars, the Pitchers have well-chosen wine lists and a changing menu which always includes their trademark: picker baskets – oriental savoury packets with various dips.

● Shampers   6 F6
4 Kingly St W1. 071-437 1692. Despite its name, wine is Shampers' most impressive feature, with over 160 different varieties from Italy, France, Germany, Australia, New Zealand, California, Chile and England. Also at least 20 champagnes, vintage port, sherries, good clarets. Downstairs is a brasserie serving international cuisine. *Closed Sat eve & all day Sun.*

● Shuffles   6 G5
3-5 Rathbone Pl W1. 071-255 1098. This basement wine bar is popular for after-work drinking. Jazz decor reigns, with large

murals of famous musicians on the walls. At *23.00 (20.00 Fri & Sat)* the wine bar becomes a night club, which is *open to 03.00.*

Smith's   7 B5
33 Shelton St WC2. 071-379 0310. Below Smith's Art Galleries, this comfortable cellar wine bar offers light snacks plus dishes from the excellent restaurant attached. *Closed Sun.*

Tall House Wine Cellar   11 F2
134 Southwark St SE1. 071-401 2929. Formerly a six-storey warehouse and now a wine cellar and art gallery on two levels, with a restaurant upstairs. *Open to 16.00. Closed Sat & Sun.*

El Vino   7 D5
47 Fleet St EC4. 071-353 6786. Something of an institution; musty atmosphere and thoroughly masculine. Little seems to change here; still a regular haunt of lawyers and journalists. Women must wear a skirt, men a jacket and tie. Spirits and liqueurs are available, also a wide range of mainly French and German wines, and about ten varieties of champagne. Sandwiches upstairs, or downstairs restaurant where it is essential to book. *Open to 20.00. Closed Sat & Sun.*

Whittington's   7 F6
21 College Hill, off Cannon St EC4. 071-248 5865. Vaulted cellars, claimed to have once belonged to Sir Richard, make an appealing wine bar on the fringe of the City. Wide-ranging wine list includes bottles from Australia, France, Germany, Spain, Italy, Portugal and Austria. *Closed Sat & Sun.*

Wine Press   6 E3
White House Hotel, Albany St NW1. 071-387 1200. Housed in the beamed cellar of a 1930s hotel. Wide range of French wines with a selection of German, Italian, Californian and Spanish bottles too. *Open to 21.00. Closed Sat & Sun (open to 10.00 for breakfast Sat & Sun only).*

INDEX

PUBS WITH RESTAURANTS

MAPS

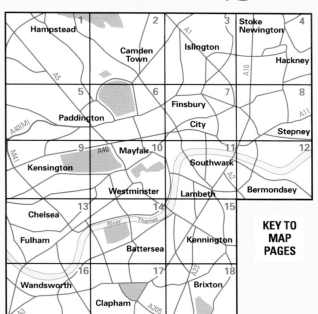

Hampstead ¹	Camden Town ²	Islington ³ A1	Stoke Newington ⁴ Hackney A10
Paddington A5 ⁵ A40(M)	⁶	Finsbury ⁷ City	⁸ A11 Stepney
Kensington M41 ⁹ A40	Mayfair ¹⁰ Westminster	Southwark ¹¹ Lambeth A3	¹² Bermondsey
Chelsea ¹³ Fulham	River Thames ¹⁴ Battersea	Kennington ¹⁵	**KEY TO MAP PAGES**
Wandsworth ¹⁶ A3	Clapham ¹⁷ A205	A23 ¹⁸ Brixton	

KEY TO MAP SYMBOLS

M41 Motorway		⊛ 🚉	British Rail Station
Dual A4 Primary Route		⬮	Underground Station
Dual A40 'A' Road		⬭	Docklands LR Station
B504 'B' Road		⬮	Bus/Coach Station
Pedestrian Street		P	Car Park

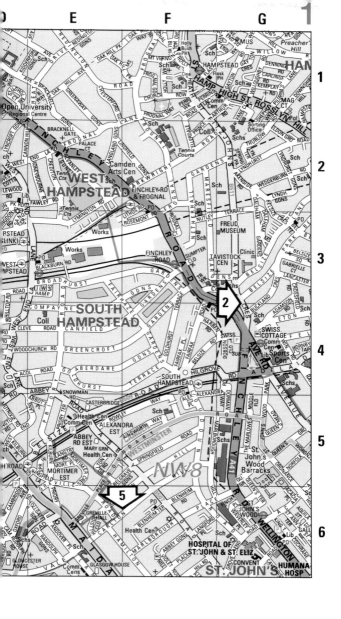

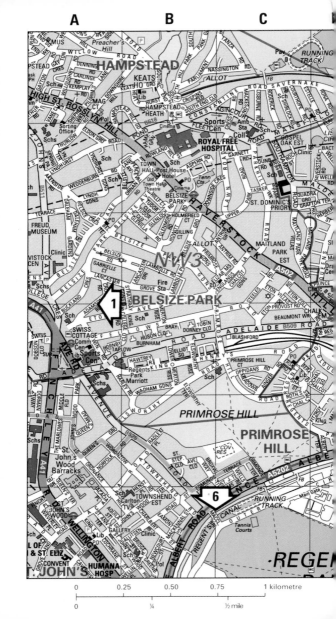

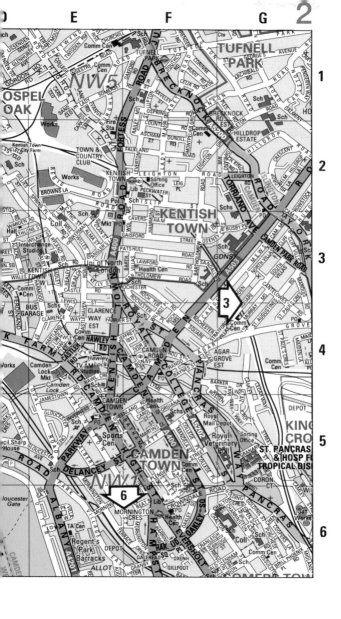

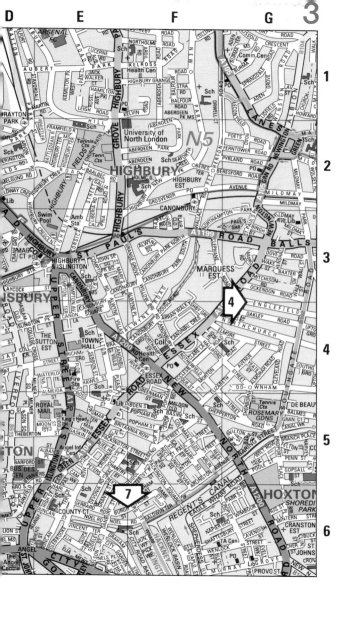

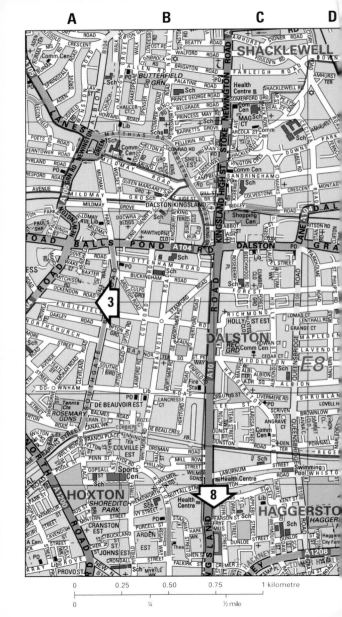

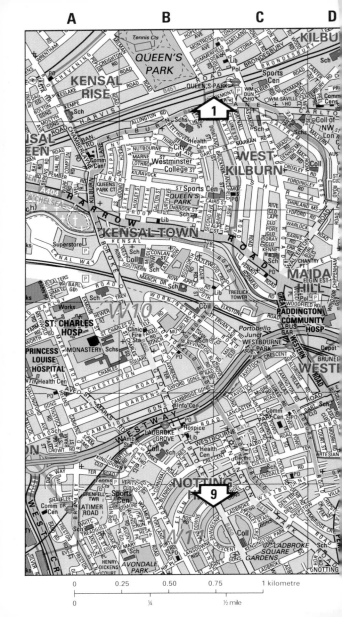

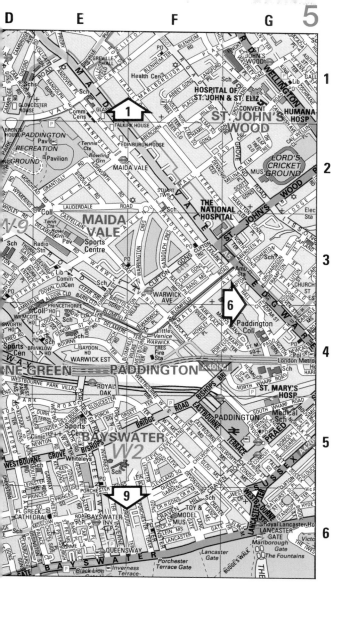

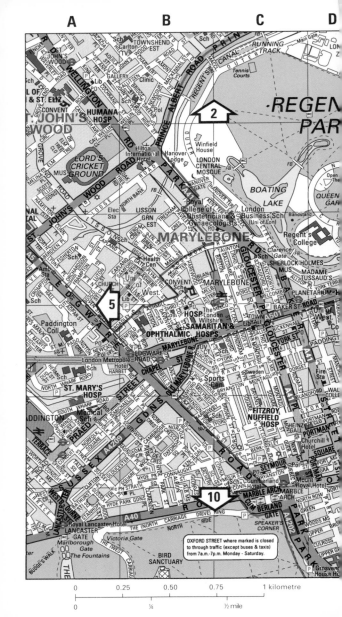

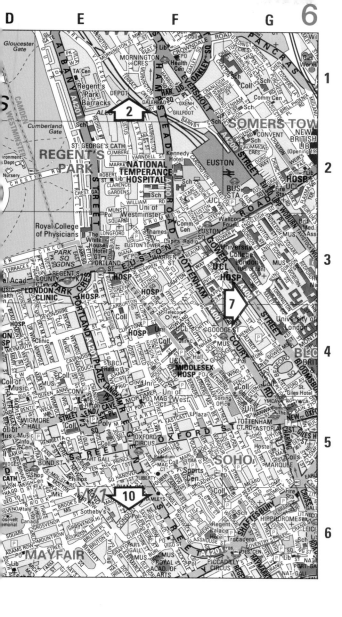

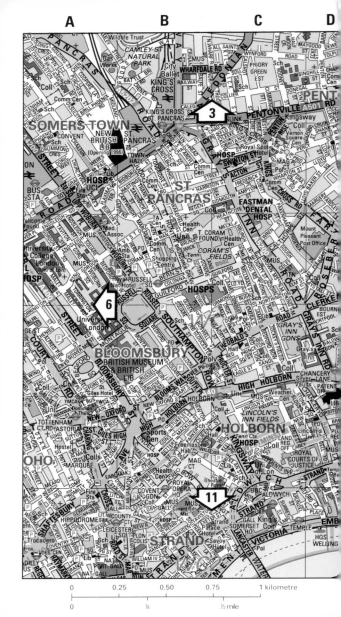

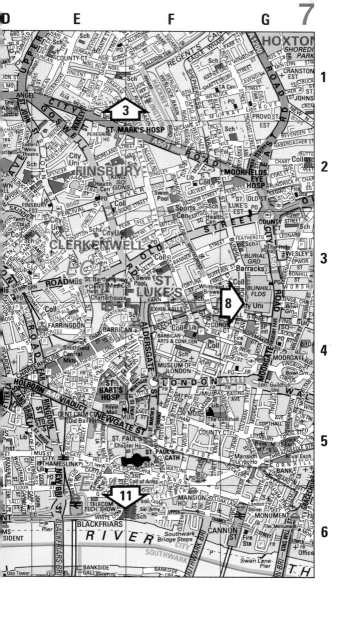

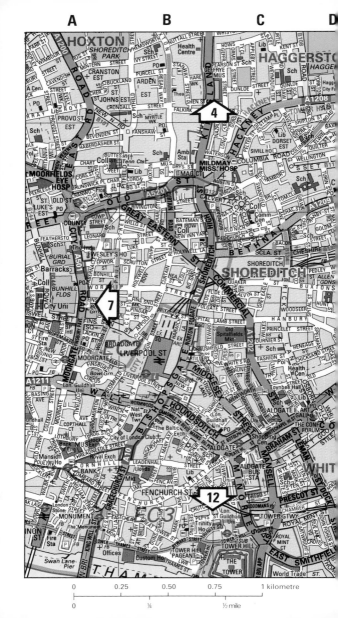

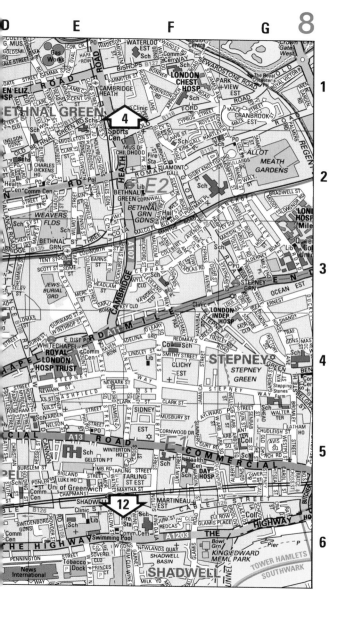

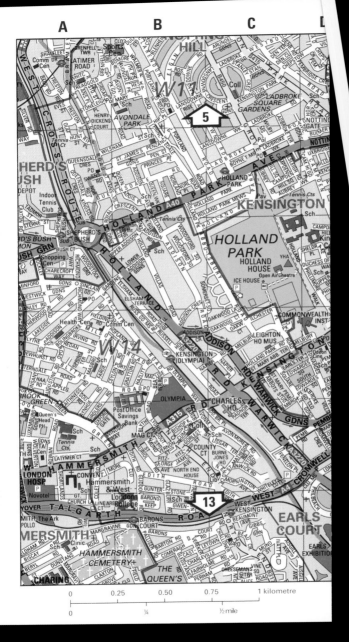

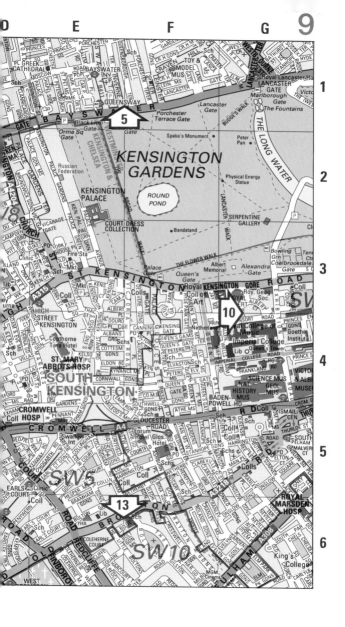

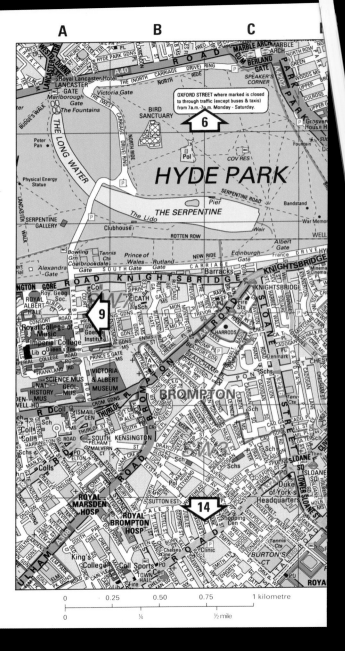

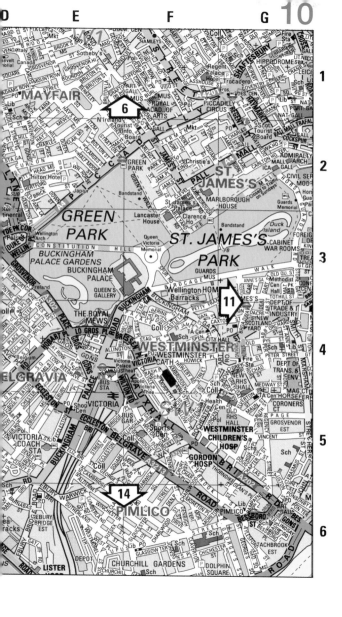

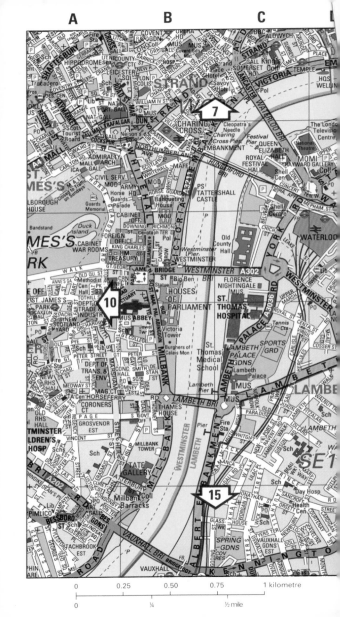

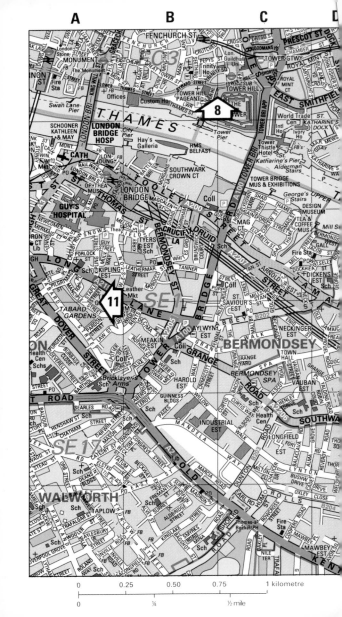

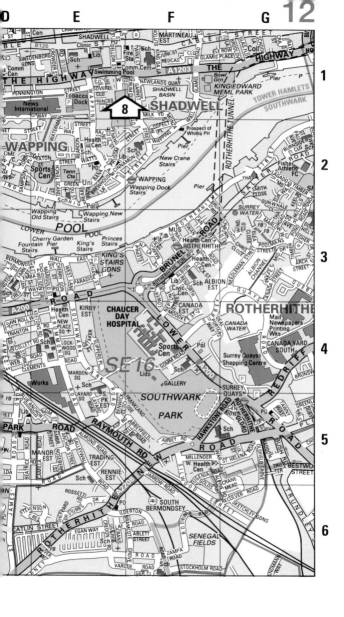

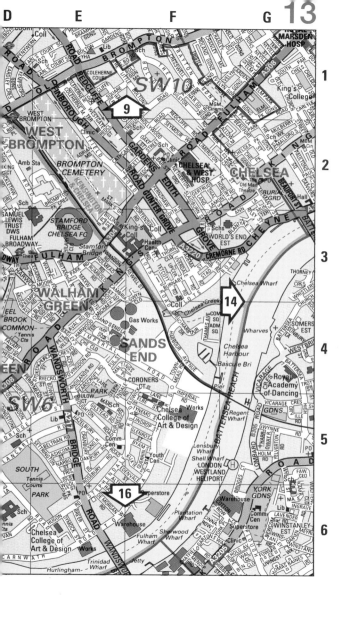

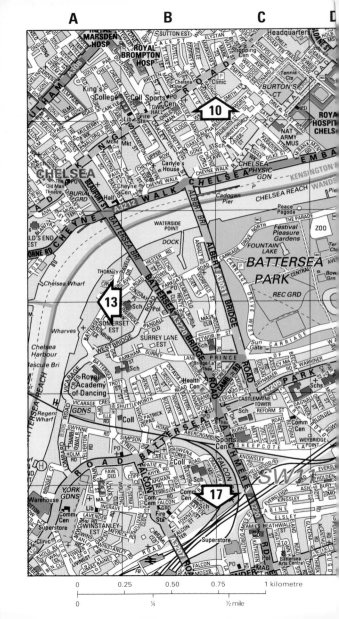

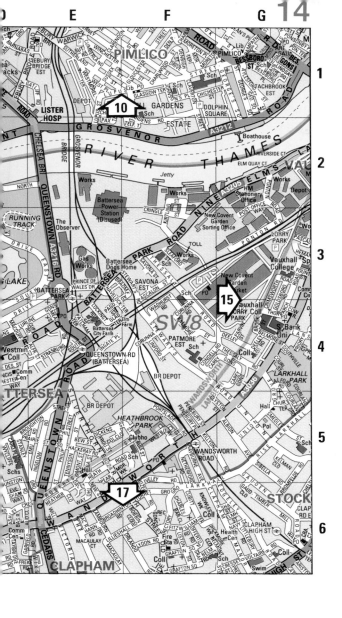

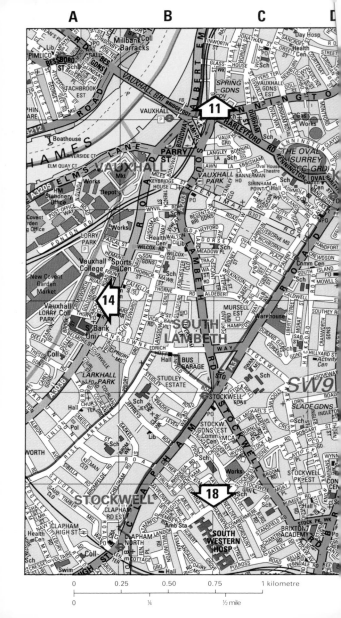

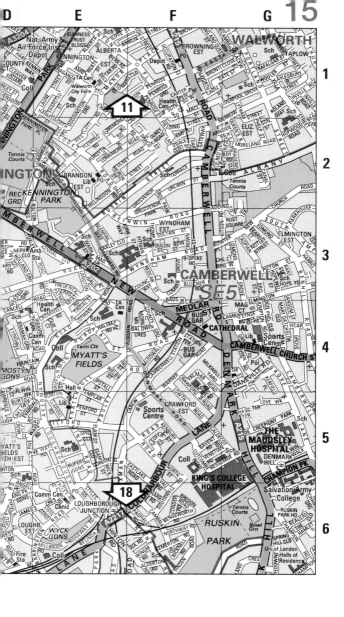

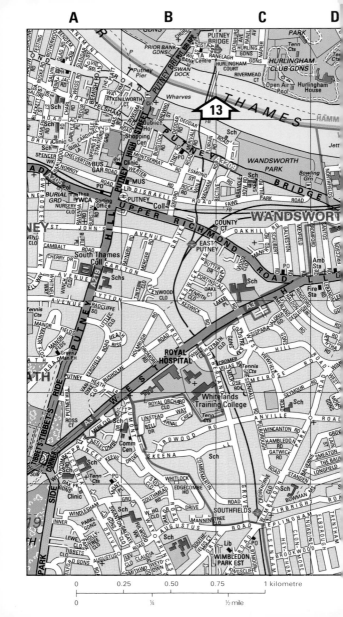

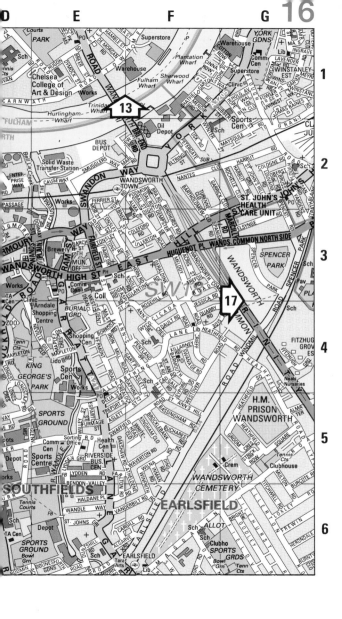

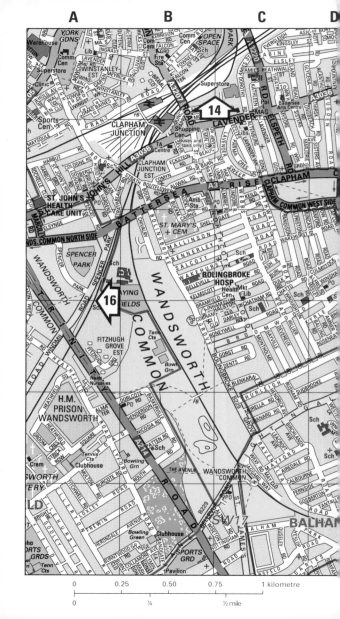

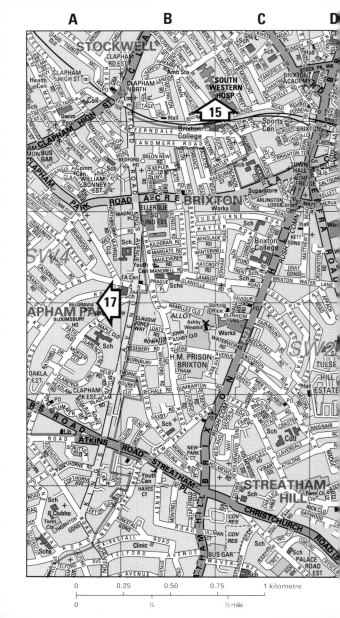

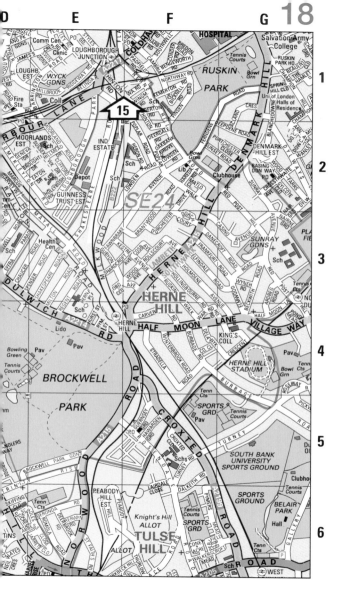

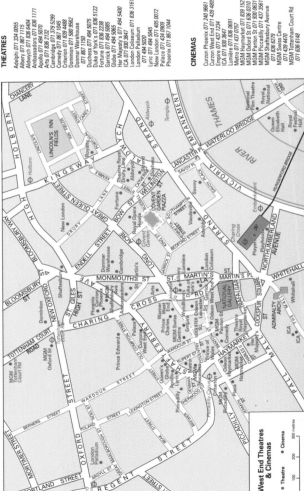

West End Theatres
& Cinemas

● Theatre   ● Cinema

0   100   200   300 metres